MW01092309

CLOUD COMPUTING

CLOUD COMPUTING
A Self-Teaching Introduction

By
RAJIV CHOPRA, PhD

MERCURY LEARNING AND INFORMATION
Dulles, Virginia
Boston, Massachusetts
New Delhi

Publisher: David Pallai

MERCURY LEARNING AND INFORMATION LLC
22841 Quicksilver Drive
Dulles, VA 20166
info@merclearning.com
www.merclearning.com
1-800-232-0223

R. Chopra. *Cloud Computing: A Self-Teaching Introduction.*
ISBN: 978-1-68392-092-2

Library of Congress Control Number: 2017934712

171819321   Printed in the USA on acid-free paper.

Our titles are available for adoption, license, or bulk purchase by institutions, corporations, etc. For additional information, please contact the Customer Service Dept. at 800-232-0223(toll free).

CONTENTS

PREFACE

Recent research has shown that cloud computing will be worth billions of dollars in new investments in the future. Organizations are migrating in large numbers to cloud services to benefit from the flexibility, self-service, abundant resources, ubiquity, responsiveness, and cost efficiencies that they offer. Many governments and private universities have already migrated to the cloud. The next wave in computing technology, expected to usher in a new era, will be based on cloud computing. This book contains state-of-the art chapters on cloud computing.

The book is chock-full of tips and insights on cloud computing and information on security and privacy. There is a plethora of books on the market today. I decided to write a book to help people understand the basic advancements in the field of cloud computing. This book also covers new and cutting edge topics that most other books miss or get subtly or blatantly wrong. The book that I have written is more practical with several case studies. I have tried to distil the value of these topics into small chunks of information. You will find a great deal of information based on research papers from several international conferences and cited journals. The theoretical items focus on explaining concepts while the practical items focus on helping you to perform a common task. A deep understanding of cloud systems is an essential element in successfully implementing these systems. We must be able to understand each new development in the cloud, assess its value, and place it in the context of our knowledge.

I love to read good books. When I open a new book on any subject, the first thing I want to know is what the book has to offer that makes it worth reading. I would like to try to help you answer that question for the book that you are holding in your hands. The facts in similar books may be the same. The difference lies in how they are presented. Believe me—while writing this book, I considered myself a student of cloud computing. The student will feel as if the teacher is sitting behind him and guiding him.

So—good luck in your endeavors!

ACKNOWLEDGMENTS

I have discovered that a major textbook project is a formidable task. Many individuals helped me to make the task manageable and kept me going.

Thanks to many colleagues who shared their ideas, experiences, and encouragement.

Numerous students, too many to name you all, also made suggestions and provided ideas. Please accept my deepest appreciation and thanks.

Finally, I would like to thanks my parents, Dr. J. R. Chopra, Mrs. Sushma Chopra, my wife Mrs. Shakti Chopra, and my twins, Arjeesh and Arshitha Chopra for their patience and blessings.

Dr. Rajiv Chopra
March 2017

CHAPTER 1

INTRODUCTION TO CLOUD COMPUTING

1.1 INTRODUCTION

Cloud computing has spawned start-ups in various new industry verticals. It has forced the existing conglomerates to acclimatize and adapt quickly to survive in such an innovative environment. It comprises a set of approaches that can help organizations quickly and effectively add and subtract resources in almost real time. Cloud computing is a business and an economic model. It is the next stage in the evolution of the Internet.

However, cloud computing is in its infancy stage. The term *cloud* in cloud computing refers to the means through which everything—from computing power to computing infrastructure, applications, business processes, and personal collaboration—can be delivered to you as a service wherever and whenever you need it [6]. A cloud is a group of interconnected network servers or PCs that may be private or public. The data and the applications served by the cloud are accessible to a group of users throughout the network. Yet, the cloud infrastructure and technology are not visible to the end users. Cloud services include the software, infrastructure, and storage delivered over the Internet based on the end users' demands. The cloud assembles large networks of virtualized services. These include *hardware services* such as compute services, storage and network, and *infrastructure services* such as web servers, databases, message queuing systems, and monitoring systems. Cloud computing is fluid in that it can expand and contract depending on the customer/business needs. From this viewpoint, the users can add or remove resources according to their needs. This quality makes cloud computing an elastic system, which can operate either manually or using automated tools.

Cloud computing is shifting computing from the physical hardware and locally managed software-enabled platforms to virtualized cloud-hosted services. Cloud providers like Microsoft Azure, Amazon Web Services (AWS), Rackspace, GoGrid, and so on, give users the option to deploy their applications over a pool of virtually infinite resources with practically no financial expenditure. It is the elasticity, cost effectiveness, and large availability of resources that force, motivate, and encourage companies to shift from enterprise applications to cloud computing.

In recent surveys conducted by different organizations, the following predictions were offered:

- Gartner Research, 2014, observed that cloud computing would be a $150 billion business.

- AMI Partners predicts SMEs (Small and Medium-sized Enterprises) are expected to spend more than $100 billion on cloud computing.

- IDC recently predicted that spending on public cloud-hosted applications would grow from $16.5 billion to over $55 billion in 2014.

- Software companies are migrating to the cloud now to reap the ultimate benefits of cloud computing.

- Recently McKinsey and Co. reported that "clouds are hardware-based services offering compute, network and storage capacity where hardware management is highly abstracted from the buyer, buyers incur infrastructure costs as variable OPEX and infrastructure capacity is highly elastic."

- In another report from the University of California, Berkeley, the key features of cloud computing are as follows:

  - The illusion of infinite computing resources.

  - The elimination of an up-front commitment by cloud users.

  - The ability to pay for use…as needed…

Principle of Cloud Computing

The principle of cloud computing is to offer computing, storage and software "as-a-service." Several researchers have given different definitions of the cloud but the basic principle is the same. Some of them are as follows:

"Cloud Computing is a paradigm in which information is permanently stored in servers on the Internet and cached temporarily on clients that include desktops, entertainment centers, table computers, notebooks, wall computers, handhelds, sensors, monitors, etc."

[Carl Hewitt, IEEE 2008]

"It is an information processing model in which centrally administered computing capabilities are delivered as services, on an as-needed basis, across the network to a variety of user-facing devices."

[Brian et al. 2014]

"It is a model for enabling convenient, on-demand network access to a shared pool of configurable computing resources (e.g., networks, servers, storage, applications and services) that can be rapidly provisioned and released with minimal management effort or service provider interaction."

[NIST, USA, 800-145]

"It is an umbrella term to describe a category of sophisticated on-demand computing services initially offered by commercial providers like Amazon, Google and Microsoft."

"It denotes a model on which a computing infrastructure is viewed as a "cloud" from which businesses and individuals access applications from anywhere in the world on demand."

"Cloud is a parallel and distributed computing system consisting of a collection of inter-connected and virtualized computers that are dynamically provisioned and presented as one or more unified computing resources based on service-level agreements (SLA) established through negotiation between the service provider and consumers."

[Buyya et al.]

"Clouds are a large pool of easily usable and accessible virtualized resources (such as hardware, development platforms and/or services). These resources can be dynamically reconfigured to adjust to a variable load (scale), allowing also for an optimum resource utilization. This pool of resources is typically exploited by a pay-per-use model in which guarantees are offered by the Infrastructure Provider by means of customized Service Level Agreements."

[Vaquero et al.]

"Data center hardware and software that provides services."

[Armbrust et al.]

"Cloud is more often used to refer to IT infrastructure deployed on an Infrastructure as a Service provider data center."

[Sotomayor et al.]

The following equation helps clarify the different parts that are combined to make up the cloud:

Hardware (virtualization of hardware, multi-core chips)
+ Internet Technologies (web services, SOA, Web 3.0)
+ Systems Management (autonomic computing)
+ Distributed Computing (grid computing, utility computing)
= The cloud

We will study these different parts later on in this chapter.

Three players (actors) make the world of cloud computing possible:

1. Vendors

2. Partners

3. Business leaders

Vendors: Provide applications and enabling technology, infrastructure, hardware, and integration.

Partners (of these vendors): Create these cloud services for the users/customers.

Business leaders: Use or evaluate these cloud computing services.

The point is that the cloud services should enable *multi-tenancy*, that is, different companies should be able to share the same available resources—online. Cloud computing cuts down on space, time, power, and cost extensively. For example, cloud services like Facebook or LinkedIn and collaboration tools such as video conferencing, document management, and webinars are affecting business functions considerably.

The cloud not only offers raw computing and storage but also software services of different types including APIs (Application Programming Interfaces) and development tools that allow web software developers to develop scalable projects.

NOTE

The ultimate goal is to run the everyday IT infrastructure in the cloud. It is possible to define this umbrella term cloud computing as "The cloud services that are made available to the users on demand via the Internet from a cloud computing provider's servers like Microsoft Azure" [Rajiv, 2016].

1.2 OVERVIEW OF PARALLEL COMPUTING

The term *parallel computing* is different from cloud computing. Parallel computing means running several computers, which may be kept in one room, but they are made to solve one problem only. Such architectures are called *advanced computer architectures* and the computers are known as *parallel computers* or *supercomputers*. These computers use parallel programming constructs; examples include the CRAY-XMP, CRAY-Y-MP, PARAGON, PARAM, and JUGENE. On the other hand, cloud computing refers to the use of resources available on the Internet via a time- and cost-effective method. This is possible due to the sharing of the resources. Thus, the cloud provides software as a service, infrastructure as a service, and platform as a service. We will discuss this in more detail later in the book.

1.3 GRID COMPUTING

Let's first consider the definition of grid computing as given in Wikipedia (the free online encyclopedia):

> Grid computing is a form of distributed computing whereby a "super and virtual computer" is composed of a cluster of networked, loosely coupled computers, acting in concert to perform very large tasks. This technology has been applied to computationally intensive scientific, mathematical and academic problems through volunteer computing and it is used in commercial enterprises for such diverse applications as drug discovery, economic forecasting, seismic analysis and back-office data processing in support of e-commerce and web services.

Grids are more loosely coupled, heterogeneous, and geographically dispersed [7]. According to Hurwitz and colleagues [6], grid computing is a step beyond distributed processing, involving large numbers of networked computers that are harnessed to solve a common problem. Clouds are usually organized as a computer grid.

According to Carl Kesselman and Ian Foster, grid computing is a cluster of computers that are geographically distributed but work together to perform a common task. In grid computing, a cluster of loosely coupled computers works together to solve a single problem that involves massive amounts of numerical calculations and compute cycles. The concept is fairly similar to that of an *electronic grid* where we can connect and use the power at any time. Grid computing uses *grid-controlling software* that divides the work into smaller pieces and assigns each piece to a pool of thousands of computers. Then later on, the controlling unit (CU) assembles the results to build the output. Thus, just as we have electronic grids to harness electric power, similarly we have grid computing to harness the power of a computer that is otherwise free.

For example, the Search for Extraterrestrial Intelligence (SETI) is a grid computing system. People all over the world share idle CPU cycles of their computers with the SETI project.

1.4 DISTRIBUTED COMPUTING AND ITS VARIANTS: MANETS, PEER-TO-PEER, AND THE CLOUD

Distributed computing refers to the different tasks that are distributed among separate nodes in the network. It includes:

- Grid computing

- Peer-to-peer architecture

- Client–server architecture

We saw what grid computing is in Section 1.3. Let's now compare peer-to-peer architecture and the cloud.

Peer-to-Peer (P2P) Architectures Compared to the Cloud

In a peer-to-peer network of hosts, resource sharing, processing, and communications control are fully decentralized. Each *host acts as a server* (provider) of some services. However, some services depend on the other nodes within the network. All clients are the same on the network. On the one hand, cloud computing is elastic and scalable in terms of resource sharing. On the other hand, peer-to-peer architectures are cheaper and simpler to manage.

Cloud computing requires a heavy initial financial investment and good technological expertise while peer-to-peer deployments have limited extensibility properties.

Client–Server Architectures Compared to the Cloud

A client–server architecture is a form of distributed computing wherein the clients depend on the number of servers that will provide them with services. Thus, its scalability involves higher costs (processing power cost, management costs, and administrative costs). On the other hand, the cloud saves money, time, and manpower. All resources are shared by the customers. There are no additional costs involved because all resources are available in the client–server architectures. In client–server deployments, a minimum of one server is a must. Thus, more costs are involved. The cloud is, therefore, cheaper.

MANETS

Ad hoc networks are formed when there is a pressing requirement to set up a network in an area. They are defined as a category of wireless networks that use multihop transmissions. They are capable of operating without any support from the existing infrastructure. Barring natural disasters, in rural areas, ad hoc networks can be set up easily. MANETS stands for Mobile Ad hoc Networks. According to the routing strategy, the routing protocols can be classified as table-driven and source-initiated protocols. On the other hand, based on the network structure, they can be classified as flat-routing, hierarchical routing, and geographical position-assisted routing protocols.

Table-Driven/Proactive Protocols: The table-driven protocols are also called *proactive protocols* because they maintain the routing information actually in advance of when it is needed. In this protocol, each and every node in the network maintains routing information to every other node in the network. In general, routing information is kept in the routing tables and is periodically updated as the network topology changes. Many of these routing protocols come from the link-state routing. Furthermore, these protocols are not suitable for larger networks because they must maintain node entries for each and every node in the routing table of every node. This leads to an increased overhead in the routing table resulting in the consumption of more bandwidth. Examples include the Fisheye State Routing Protocol (FSR) and the Optimized Link

State Routing Protocol (OLSR), as well as some on-demand routing protocols/ reactive protocols.

On-demand Routing Protocols/Reactive Protocols: These are called *reactive protocols* because they do not maintain routing information or routing activity in the network nodes if there is no communication. If a node wants to send a packet to another node then this protocol searches for the route in an on-demand manner and establishes the connection in order to transmit and receive the packet. The route discovery occurs by flooding the route request packets throughout the network. Examples include Dynamic Source Routing (DSR) and Ad-hoc On-demand Distance Vector (AODV) Routing.

MANETS can also use Hierarchical State Routing (HSR) protocols. This protocol maintains a hierarchical topology where elected cluster heads at the lowest level become members of the next higher level. At the higher level, super clusters are formed. The nodes that want to communicate to a node outside of their cluster ask their cluster head to forward their packet to the next level, until a cluster head of the other node is in the same cluster. Then the packet travels down to the destination node. HSR proposes to cluster nodes in a logical way rather than in a geographical way.

They can use Zone Routing Protocols (ZRP). This is also known as a hybrid reactive/proactive routing protocol. As the name implies, ZRP is based on the concept of zones. A routing zone is defined for each node separately and the zones of the neighboring nodes overlap. The routing zone has a radius expressed in hops. Thus, the zone includes the nodes whose distance from the node in question has the most hops. The number of nodes in the routing zone can be regulated by adjusting the transmission power of the nodes. Furthermore, lowering the power reduces the number of nodes within direct reach and vice versa. The number of neighboring nodes should be sufficient to provide adequate reach ability and redundancy. On the other hand, a too large coverage results in many zone members and the update traffic becomes excessive.

MANETS may also use geographic position-assisted routing. It includes protocols like Location-Aided Routing (LAR) and Distance Routing Effect Algorithm for Mobility (DREAM).

MANETS is a collection of mobile nodes with no pre-established or fixed architecture. Network nodes act as routers by relaying each other's packets. It is a wireless network in which nodes communicate through a single hop or multi-hop paths. MANETS have dynamic topologies, bandwidth constraints, variable capacity links, and self-organized behavior.

1.5 INTRODUCTION TO AUTONOMIC COMPUTING

Let's first of all define an autonomic system. The term *autonomic* is derived from the concept of biology. We say autonomous systems are those that monitor changes that affect the body and are based on the human autonomic nervous system. Say you touch a hot plate or anything hot, and then suddenly you remove your hands from the heat. This happens because nerves send messages to the brain to immediately move your hands away from the heat. This action occurs automatically. Thus, such systems are self-managing. In the field of computer science, we also have the concept of autonomic computing. Such systems should be able to handle events autonomously like malicious attacks, hardware and software faults, power shutdowns, software updates, and so on. IBM introduced the concept of autonomic systems with the following features:

1. **Self-Awareness:** They know themselves very well.

2. **Self-Configuring:** The system should be able to configure and reconfigure itself under varying conditions.

3. **Self-Optimizing:** The system should be able to optimize itself to improve its execution.

4. **Self-Healing:** The system should be able to detect and correct problems and to continue functioning.

5. **Self-Protecting:** The system should be able to protect itself from both internal and external security attacks.

6. **Open Systems:** The system should be developed using standard and open protocols and interfaces.

The basic concept of autonomic systems is their self-management. The objective of an autonomous self-healing process is to keep the elements working according to their design specifications.

In a nutshell, we could say that, "it is a set of self-managing, self-healing, self-configuration, self-optimization, and self-protection, features of distributed computing resources that operate on the basis of a set of pre-defined policies."

1.6 HISTORICAL DEVELOPMENT AND EVOLUTION OF CLOUD COMPUTING

History of the Cloud

Initially cloud computing was thought of as being only public. Thus, it was called the public cloud. However, due to security reasons, we shifted from public clouds to private clouds. The focus was toward making the cloud more secure and yet to provide the same services and resource sharing. Then cloud infrastructures naturally evolved to what is known as hybrid clouds. Hybrid clouds can be explained with the help of an equation also:

$$\text{Hybrid Cloud} = \text{Public Cloud} + \text{Private Cloud}$$

This means that now you can have the benefits of both internal network storage as well as public data clouds that can be accessed from anywhere in the world using the Internet. Using broadband services along with the cloud, companies can connect to larger networks to make use of available resources. There is no need for a huge computer now to handle complex tasks like database indexing.

Evolution of the Cloud

In the 1960s:

(a) Joseph Licklider, a Professor at MIT, described the idea of cloud computing and resource sharing.

(b) Professor John McCarthy, at MIT and Stanford focused on the concepts of time-sharing, computing power, and applications being used and sold as a utility and online social networking.

(c) In 1966, Douglas F. Parkhill, published a book on *The Challenge of Computer Utility* wherein he described the utility-like features of cloud computing such as dynamic provisioning, illusion of infinite supply, and being always online.

In the 1970s:

(a) In 1979, Dun and Bradstreet bought National CSS, which sold the time-sharing concept.

(b) BBN Technologies, founded by MIT, in the 1970s marketed time-sharing.

In the 1980s:

(a) In 1985, DEC also introduced VAX clusters where several VAX machines were grouped together for resource sharing.

(b) In 1980, Tim Berners-Lee worked on hypertext and is known today as the father of the Internet.

NOTE *All these advancements were pre-cloud phases of cloud development.*

In the 1990s:

(a) Ian Foster and Carl Kesselman wrote a book entitled The Grid: Blueprint for a New Computing Infrastructure. They explain the concepts of grid computing, which can work cohesively for computationally intensive tasks.

(b) In 1998, the Data Protection Act in the UK had a very long-term impact on cloud computing. This act covered data collection, protection, and sharing in a multi-tenant environment.

(c) In 1999, Salesforce.com, who happens to be a pioneer in Software-as-a-Service (SaaS) CRM, made the cloud operational.

(d) In the mid-1990s, Yahoo also offered cloud-based email services.

(e) Again in the 1990s, server virtualization was introduced (based on 8086 microprocessors). This became the base/foundation for cloud resource sharing.

(f) In 1998, VMware was founded by Mendel and colleagues at the University of California.

In the 2000s:

(a) In 2001, the SIIA (Software and Information Industry Association) used the acronym SaaS and compared it with ASP (Application Service Provider).

(b) In 2002, Amazon launched its web services to permit users to integrate their websites with Amazon's online content. This later became IaaS, EC2 (Elastic Compute Cloud), and S3 (Storage-as-a-Service). They actually introduced pay-per-use pricing and very quickly it became a standard with other companies.

(c) In 2003, Nicholas Carr, published a research paper in the Harvard Business Review called "IT Doesn't Matter" wherein he described that corporate will start purchasing IT resources as and when needed from external resources only.

(d) In 2008, Gartner declared cloud computing an emerging technology that was still in its infancy stage.

1.7 VISION OF CLOUD COMPUTING

Cloud computing can save money and time. This is the major goal of the cloud. Big companies who provide their customers with cloud services also provide SLAs, that is, Service Level Agreements.

We define an SLA as a contract in which the service providing companies agree on a specified level of service (or uptime). An SLA gives potential customers a sort of confidence in using cloud computing services. The system administrator has a role. They should ensure that the uptime is constant. They can easily achieve this because of the redundancy of cloud computing. Several SLAs promote an uptime level of 99.999% but cannot always provide for data redundancy to be commensurate. This problem can be solved by making sure that data integrity is written into the SLA agreement itself to prevent any kind of confusion.

1.8 PROPERTIES AND CHARACTERISTICS OF CLOUD COMPUTING

Some of the key characteristics of cloud computing are as follows:

1. Cloud service providers like MS Azure, Amazon Web Service (AWS), IBM, and Google provide on-demand self-services. The cloud includes a

set of approaches that can help organizations quickly and effectively add and subtract resources in almost real time.

2. Cloud services can even be used on mobile phones. Thus, they have a broader network access.

3. Resources like memory, network bandwidth, and virtual machines can be easily shared now, and according to Gartner, pooling resources like this builds economies to a large extent. The cloud also focuses on maximizing the effectiveness of the shared resources. Cloud resources are usually not only shared by multiple users, but are also dynamically reallocated per demand. This can work for allocating resources to users. Furthermore, with cloud computing, multiple users can access a single server to retrieve and update their data without purchasing licenses for different applications.

4. The cloud is elastic. This means that if needed you can easily scale in or scale out resources.

5. It is possible to measure, manage, and control cloud computing resource practices. The cloud works on a "pay-as-you-go" principle just as our electricity meters work. Thus, you are charged only for the time you are using cloud services.

6. Multi-tenancy is another feature of the cloud. It refers to different companies sharing the same underlying resources.

7. The cloud adopted features from SOA (Service-Oriented Architecture) that can help the user break these problems into services that can be then integrated to provide a solution. Cloud computing provides all of its resources as services and makes use of well-established standards.

8. Cloud computing is a marketing term. It refers to a model of network computing where a program or application runs on a connected server or servers rather than on a local computing device like a PC, tablet, or smart phone.

9. Like a traditional client–server model or legacy mainframe computing, a user connects with a server to perform a task. The difference with cloud computing is that the computing process may run on one or many connected computers at the same time, utilizing the concept of virtualization.

10. Cloud computing is not a quick fix solution. It requires considerable thought before implementing it in an organization.

11. It requires a strong foundation of best practices in software development, software architecture, and service management foundations.

12. It is user-centric, task-centric, document-centric, powerful, accessible, intelligent, and programmable.

13. Cloud computing is not network computing. Nor is it traditional outsourcing.

14. It should facilitate a shift from remote data to current data, from applications to tasks and from computer to the user, with the objective of access from any place and sharing it with anyone. Authorized users have instant access.

15. The cloud when used with IT will be more beneficial than when used in isolation.

1.9 REFERENCE MODEL FOR CLOUD COMPUTING

There are three major models of cloud computing services and they are known as *Software-as-a-Service (SaaS), Platform-as-a-Service (PaaS), and Infrastructure-as-a-Service (IaaS)*. These cloud services may be offered in a public, private, or hybrid network [NIST]. Some of the cloud vendors include MS Azure, Amazon, IBM, Oracle Cloud, Salesforce, and Google.

For example, Windows Azure is Microsoft's cloud-based application platform for developing, managing, and hosting applications off site. MS Azure consists of several components such as the cloud operating system itself, SQL Azure (which provides database services in the cloud) and .NET services. Azure runs on computers that are physically located in Microsoft data centers. We will discuss these data centers a bit later.

Let's now compare the three service models as shown in Table 1.1.

TABLE 1.1 Cloud Computing Service Models

Model	Explanations	Examples
IaaS	The customer gets resources such as processing power, storage, network bandwidth, CPU, and power. Once the user gets the infrastructure, he controls the OS, data, applications, services, host-based security, and so on.	Amazon Web Services (AWS), RackSpace, GoGrid, Verizon, IBM, and AT&T.
PaaS	The customer is provided with the hardware infrastructure, network, and operating system to form a hosting environment. The user can install his applications and activate services from the hosting environment.	MS Azure, Google App Engine, Force.com, Informatica onDemand, Keynote Systems, Caspio, Tibco, and WaveMaker.
SaaS	The customer/user is provided access to an application. He has no control over the hardware, network, security, or OS.	Salesforce.com, Google, MS, Ramco, and Zoho.

We will discuss these service models in detail in Chapter 2. However, cloud services are typically made available via public, private, or hybrid clouds. Let's define these and compare them first.

I. Public Cloud/External Cloud: In general, these clouds offer services over the Internet and are owned and operated by a cloud provider. For example, email services, social networking sites, and so on, are all aimed at the general public. The following points characterize public clouds (or external clouds):

1. They offer services to users on the principle of pay-by-use (explained earlier).

2. They are run by third parties because they require a huge investment to build.

3. In this model, applications from different customers are mixed together on storage systems, cloud servers, and other infrastructures within the cloud.

4. The customers can choose a location to deploy the application. This mitigates latency, risks, time, and costs for the users.

5. Data control and security are important tasks here.

6. The public cloud is always larger than an organization's private cloud because it provides the ability to scale up and down and to transfer the risks of an infrastructure from an organization to the cloud provider.

7. This cloud is a better choice if the standardized workload for an application is used by several people, you need to test and develop application code, or if you have SaaS applications from a cloud vendor. It may be a good choice if you need incremental capacity, that is, to add compute capacity at peak times, if you are using collaboration projects, or even if you are doing an ad hoc software development.

8. In this type of cloud, the service providers charge the companies according to their usage.

9. Here, resources are owned or hosted by the cloud service providers (company) and the services are sold to other companies (Figure 1.1).

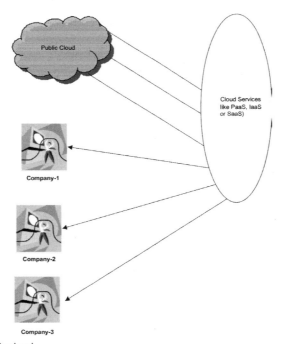

FIGURE 1.1 TA public cloud.

10. No direct connectivity is provided by public cloud service providers like Amazon AWS, MS, and Google.

II. Private Cloud/Internal Cloud: Just as a public cloud can be thought of as Internet, similarly, a private cloud can be thought of as an intranet. The following points characterize private or internal clouds:

1. A private cloud or internal cloud is used when the data center in the cloud is to be operated only for a specific business.

2. It serves the client with maximum security, quality of service, and data control.

3. The infrastructure is owned by the company and it has power over how applications are deployed on it.

4. With private clouds, the IT infrastructure of organizations can be merged. This mitigates the electricity bill as well.

5. They are limited to the organizational boundary.

6. They can be set up from MS, IBM, VMware, Eucalyptus, OpenStack, and so on.

7. They are used when the security of your organization is of paramount importance.

8. Your company has so much potential, in terms of money, that it can run even a next generation cloud data center most efficiently and effectively.

9. The cloud computing infrastructure that is designed only for a single company cannot be shared with other organizations.

10. They are more expensive and secure.

11. The main objective of a private cloud is not to sell cloud services to external organizations but to exploit the benefits of a cloud architecture by denying the rights to manage your data center to outsiders.

12. Private clouds are virtual distributed systems that depend only on private infrastructure.

13. They provide internal users with dynamic provisioning of computing resources.

14. Therefore, security concerns are less critical here.

15. Testing a private cloud is cheaper than testing a public cloud.

16. The problem is that private clouds cannot scale out easily in case of heavy (peak) demands (Figure 1.2).

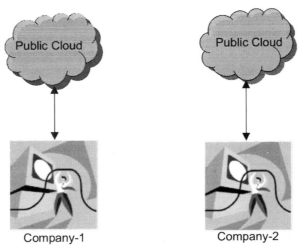

FIGURE 1.2 Private clouds.

To cope with all of these problems, the only solution is to combine both public and private clouds to achieve a hybrid cloud.

Before we discuss hybrid clouds further, we can review the differences between public and private clouds in Table 1.2.

TABLE 1.2 Differences between Public and Private Clouds

Public Cloud	Private Cloud
1. Its owner is the cloud provider or third party.	1. Its owner is solely the organization.
2. It involves lower costs.	2. It involves more costs.
3. Scalability is on demand and unlimited.	3. Scalability is limited to the infrastructure installed.

4. Less security.	4. Higher security.
5. Testing it is difficult because every-thing is public.	5. Testing is easier because it is a private cloud.
6. Performance is difficult to achieve.	6. Its performance is guaranteed.
7. Less management and control is needed because it works on the con-cept of virtualization.	7. More management and control is needed because it has a higher level of control over resources.

A Variant on a Private Cloud

A community cloud is a type/variant of a private cloud but it goes beyond a business or an organization. It is implemented when several businesses have similar requirements and perspectives to share. They are accessible to members of a particular community but are not available to the general public.

Examples include branches of educational organizations and government, military, and industry suppliers.

The following points characterize community clouds:

1. They are needed when there is a necessity for general services.

2. By creating virtual machines from the machines that are underutilized, a community cloud can be established (see Figure 1.3).

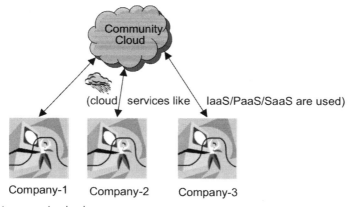

FIGURE 1.3 A community cloud.

Now let's study hybrid clouds.

Hybrid Clouds/Mixed Clouds: Here, the focus was to make clouds more secure and yet to provide the same services and resource sharing. Thus, cloud infrastructures naturally evolved to what is known as *hybrid clouds*. Hybrid/ mixed clouds can be explained with the help of an equation also:

$$\text{Hybrid Cloud} = \text{Public Cloud} + \text{Private Cloud}$$

This means that now you can have the benefits of both internal network storage as well as public data clouds that can be accessed from anywhere in the world using the Internet. Using broadband services along with the cloud, companies can connect to larger networks to make use of available resources. There is no need of a huge computer to handle complex tasks like database indexing. The following points characterize hybrid clouds:

1. Better scalability and reliability because they allow companies to move from public to private clouds.

2. Better sharing of resources on demand.

3. It is an approach for extending the infrastructure beyond the organizational firewall with more security.

4. Applications that are more important are stored on a hybrid cloud, but less important applications and data are stored on a public cloud.

5. An example of hybrid usage would be a patient's record or some financial matters that cannot be put on public cloud servers because it is sensitive information. These scenarios can make use of hybrid clouds.

6. This type of cloud is used during cloud bursting. In this case, an organization generally uses its own computing infrastructure but in case of higher load requirements, the company can access the cloud. This means that the company using a hybrid cloud can manage an internal cloud/private cloud for its general usage and it can migrate the entire application to the public cloud during heavy peak hours.

7. This is shown in a diagram in Figure 1.4.

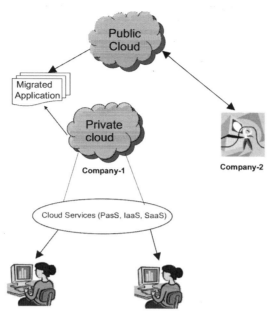

FIGURE 1.4 Hybrid clouds.

8. The purpose is to lease public cloud services when private cloud capacity is insufficient.

9. B. Sotomayor et al. states that "a hybrid cloud takes shape when a private cloud is supplemented with computing capacity from public clouds. This method of temporarily renting a capacity to handle spikes in load is known as cloud bursting."

10. We can combine a private cloud with a public cloud or even a public one with community clouds.

11. A comparison of public clouds and community clouds is shown in Table 1.3.

TABLE 1.3 Public Clouds versus Community Clouds

Public Cloud	Community Cloud
1. Any user who signs up can use a public cloud.	1. Only users within a particular industry segment/group can use it. These users have common objectives.

2. It employs a pay-per-use model, which is expensive.	2. It is more expensive because the site is customized for use by the company group.
3. Security is lower.	3. More secure because a limited number of users have accounts.
4. The provider is not known to the consumer.	4. The provider is not known to the consumer.
5. Compliance with regulations is not an objective of the organization.	5. The objective is to have compliance with the regulations of an organization.

12. Similarly, we can compare a private cloud and a hybrid cloud (Table 1.4).

TABLE 1.4 Private Cloud versus Hybrid Cloud

Private Cloud	Hybrid Cloud
1. It is fully set up by a company.	1. It uses the resources of a public provider on a pay-per-use model.
2. Performance is limited.	2. More scalable and elastic because it can use public resources to meet load spikes.
3. Less flexible.	3. More flexible because it can develop and test services on a public cloud and later deploy them on a private cloud.
4. More expensive.	4. It is cheaper.

1.10 CLOUD COMPUTING ENVIRONMENTS

According to a report by Dell in 2012, the cloud is not just a technology. Rather, it is a corporate strategy based on business outcomes. The real benefit of the cloud comes when it is integrated with IT and leveraged across all environments. The service consultants should work to understand the business and help customers to plan, build, deploy, manage, and access clouds that meet their specific needs. Furthermore, it is necessary to create virtualization or visualization environments and develop and implement the application on cloud platforms.

The NIST Cloud Computing Standards Roadmap Working Group (NIST-SP 500-292 std.), an agency of the U.S. Department of Commerce, has surveyed the existing standards landscape for security, portability, and inter-operability standards/models/studies/use cases, and so on, relevant to cloud computing. The overview of the Reference Architecture for the cloud lists five major actors: cloud consumer, cloud provider, cloud broker, cloud auditor, and cloud carrier [NIST Executive Summary].

We have already seen the role of a cloud provider. However, a cloud auditor has the job of security and privacy audit. A cloud broker has the job of service intermediation and service aggregation.

NIST also identified three deployment models: public cloud, private cloud, and hybrid clouds. The main differences between each are based on how exclusive the computing services and resources are for the cloud consumer.

1.11 CLOUD SERVICES REQUIREMENTS

Here we list some of the best practices that every successful cloud computing platform should follow:

1. **Better Security:** Providing the best security at every level.

2. **Better Transparency:** Providing transparent, real-time, accurate service performance and information.

3. **True Multi-tenancy:** Deliver maximum scalability and performance to customers with a true multi-tenant architecture.

4. **Proven Scale:** Support millions of users with proven scalability.

5. **Better Performance:** Deliver consistent, high-speed performance globally.

6. **Better Disaster Recovery:** Protect customer data by running the service on multiple geographically dispersed data centers with extensive backup, data archive, and failover capabilities.

7. **Better Availability:** Equip world-class facilities with proven high-availability infrastructure and application software.

8. **Resource Reservation:** The cloud should assure that at the needed time, the resources or the services will be absolutely available to the customer.

9. **Self-Service portal:** The cloud should offer a self-service facility to its customers. Similar to McDonalds, if there is no one to serve you a cheeseburger, then you opt for self-service. Similarly, cloud users should be able to manage using a web-based self-service portal.

10. **Dynamic Resource Allocations:** It should be possible through the cloud to perform resource distribution and re-distributions easily. This dynamic resource allocation and de-allocation illustrates the efficiency of SaaS.

11. The resource distribution and actual cloud utilization must be reported in an accounting database.

12. Dynamic workload management, resource automation, and metering of these resources are also required essentials in a cloud.

1.12 THE CLOUD AND DYNAMIC INFRASTRUCTURE

We define a dynamic infrastructure as an information technology paradigm that concerns the design of data centers so that the underlying hardware and software can respond dynamically to changing levels of demand in more fundamental and efficient ways than before. This paradigm is also known as *Infrastructure 2.0* and a *Next Generation Data Center*.

Principle of Dynamic Infrastructures

The principle of dynamic infrastructures is "To leverage pooled IT resources to provide flexible IT capacity, enabling seamless, real-time allocation of IT resources in line with demand from business processes." This is achieved using server virtualization technology to pool computing resources wherever possible and allocating these resources on demand using automated tools. This provides load balancing because it avoids underutilization of resources.

Examples include Flex Frame for SAP, which is a server-level dynamic infrastructure (or e.g., Flex Frame for Oracle Solutions by Fujitsu Siemens Computers).

Fujitsu defines dynamic infrastructures as enabling customers to assign IT resources dynamically to services as required and to choose sourcing models which best fit their businesses. This brings IT flexibility and efficiency to the next level.

IBM defines dynamic infrastructures as integrating business and IT assets and aligning them with the overall goals of the business while taking a smarter, new, and more streamlined approach to helping improve service, reduce cost, and manage risk.

The approach of these companies is to dynamically assign servers to applications on demand, leveling peaks, and enabling companies to maximize the benefit of their IT investments, that is, their Return-on-Investment (ROI). If an enterprise switches to dynamic infrastructures, then it also reduces costs, improves quality-of-service, and make more important use of energy by reducing the number of standby or underutilized machines in their data centers. Furthermore, these dynamic infrastructures provide for failover from a smaller pool of spare machines. By reducing redundant capacity, organizations are enabled to make more efficient use of their IT budgets and devote greater proportions of their budget to physical and virtual production servers.

Dynamic infrastructures may also be used to provide security and data protection when workloads are moved during migrations, provisioning, enhancing performance, or building co-location facilities.

Benefits of Dynamic Infrastructures :

- Enhancing performance
- Scalability
- System availability and uptime
- Better server utilizations
- Performing routine maintenance of physical or virtual systems
- Mitigating interruption to business operations
- Reducing IT costs
- Providing business continuity

For networking companies, Infrastructure 2.0 refers to the ability of networks to keep up with the movement and scale requirements of new enterprise

IT initiatives, like virtualization and cloud computing. As per the reports of big companies like Cisco, F5 Networks, and Infoblox, network automation and connectivity intelligence between networks, applications, and endpoints will be required to reap the full benefits of virtualization and cloud computing. This requires network management and infrastructure to consolidate, enabling higher levels of dynamic control and connectivity between networks, systems, and endpoints.

Uses of Dynamic Infrastructures

Dynamic infrastructures make use of the intelligence gained across the network. By design, every dynamic infrastructure is service-oriented. It can also use alternative sourcing approaches like cloud computing to deliver new services with agility and speed.

Dynamic Infrastructure Applications

1. Transportation companies can optimize their vehicle's routes leveraging GPS and traffic information.

2. Technology systems can be optimized for energy efficiency, managing spikes in demand, and ensuring disaster recovery readiness.

3. Utility companies can reduce energy with a "smart grid."

Gartner et al. reports that:

1. Virtualized applications can reduce the cost of testing, packaging, and supporting an application by 60% and that they reduced overall TCO by 5% to 7% in their model.

2. Green issues are the primary driver in 10% of current data center outsourcing and hosting initiatives. Cost reduction initiatives are a driver of 47% of the time and are now aligned well with green goals. Furthermore, combining these two means that at least 57% of data center outsourcing and hosting initiatives are driven by going green.

3. They also report that by 2013, more than 50% of midsize organizations and more than 75% of large enterprises will implement layered recovery architectures.

1.13 CLOUD ADOPTION

No doubt, a company can adopt the cloud because it has many benefits, but at the same time, it has some drawbacks as well. Why are organizations moving today toward cloud computing? Some of the benefits of this movement are as follows:

1. Reduced organizational cost (a pay-as-you-go model is used)
2. Better storage
3. More automation
4. Better flexibility
5. Better mobility
6. Better IT personnel utilization
7. More security
8. Better investment
9. Better service
10. No need for software installations
11. Shorter deployment times needed
12. Better Customer Relationship Management (CRM)

The cloud allows businesses and people to avail themselves of services and information available from any place at any time as long as the system is in the network. Practically speaking, we all use different types of cloud services in different ways in our daily life; for example, Gmail, Pandora (music website), and so on.

The cloud should also be innovative with regard to the different cloud actors, as discussed earlier. Cloud adoption follows a life cycle:

Phase-1: (Evaluation) Evaluate cloud challenges, prospects, and the impact on markets.

Phase-2: (Plan) Build up a cloud strategy, develop and implement security measures, plan for which service to implement in a company (out of SaaS, IaaS, or PaaS).

Phase-3: (Adopt) After planning, we can contemplate cloud adoption, keeping in mind various cloud deployment architectures and identifying the servers to understand its implementation.

Phase-4: (Optimize) Deliver online lessons after every cloud deployment in an organization. Draw timeline charts and locate skilled people before you deploy a cloud.

The selection of cloud computing strategies for an organization involves very critical issues. The question is to see where, if a company adopts a cloud technology, it will give any value to the present business? How much effort and risk is involved in a cloud implementation? Can we implement the cloud on only a few selected areas of the business? How can we control the shifting of an organization from current technology to cloud computing? It is also important to understand that the answer to this is that the organization should make a decision to implement the cloud on the basis of three factors, that is, scalability, availability, and cost and convenience. The term Cloud Data Center (CDC) is also in the cloud computing literature. A CDC may be an internal, external, or a federated provider of infrastructure, platform, or software services.

However, an optimal decision cannot always be established for all cases. This is because the types of resources (infrastructure, storage, software) obtained from a CDC depend on the size of the organization and an understanding of the IT impact on business, workloads, flexibility, and available money and resources for testing. The objective is to have a scalability-driven, availability-driven, market-driven, and convenience-driven strategy.

1.14 ISSUES AND CHALLENGES IN CLOUD COMPUTING

Some of the major cloud issues and challenges are as follows:

1. Cloud security is of paramount importance today. This is because data is shared on the cloud and this makes the data as well as the information more vulnerable to cloud cyber attacks. Ambrust et al. state that current cloud offerings are essentially public...exposing the system to more attacks."

2. The absence of better quality services in a cloud can make organizations decline.

3. The cloud should provide better inter-operability and portability because the industry truly needs it.

4. Resource sharing and complex data on the net needs sufficient bandwidth. More costs are involved. This is not acceptable to many companies.

5. A cloud can regularly experience failures. Cloud reliability means a failure-free operation of the cloud. Unfortunately, this happens to be a very big issue.

6. Parallel data access by multiple customers at all times and a mix of hardware types means data protection in any cloud becomes very complex. The data must be made redundant/duplicated/replicated and stored at different locations, and it should be easily accessible. However, having data redundancy means also having a check on data location, latency, user workload, backup, report generation, application testing, and so on. Thus, data redundancy is not an easy task.

7. Cloud disaster recovery is very important when we evaluate cloud providers.

8. An issue also arises when you back up cloud data; for example, if you download data on your pen drives, you need to pay for the bandwidth. Another issue arises when you need to save data to a more secure location.

9. Data recovery to a cloud-based service site is challenging, slow, and prone to errors. This occurs more when you upload a large amount of data to the cloud over a WAN connection.

10. Consumers of cloud services are not aware of where the primary or replicated data copies reside. User data is usually distributed across many data centers. Furthermore, a company's cloud data may not reside within the operating or registered country.

11. Service reliability is also a bigger challenge given hardware and software components that are heterogeneous, connectivity that is over multi-vendor WANs, and user-friendliness, for example.

12. Several users work simultaneously on different data sets in the cloud. Thus, the data is split or fragmented into many pieces and stored in various storage locations. This is called data fragmentation. This

data spreading leads to inefficiency and reduces the read/write performances.

13. Data integration is itself a challenge because data that has been distributed over different data centers cannot be easily integrated.

14. Cloud data can be accessed only when both the user and the services are online. This access requires bandwidth, which further depends on the size of the workload.

15. Data transformation is also an issue. The process of converting the cloud data format into a format that can be easily used by other cloud applications is known as data transformation. This is an issue because the transformed data may not be compatible with different environments. Additionally, data transformation creates multiple copies and managing these is a big issue.

16. Cloud standardization is also an issue today. The Cloud Computing Interoperability Forum (CCIF) was formed by various companies including Intel, Sun, and Cisco to enable a global cloud computing ecosystem whereby organizations would be able to seamlessly work together for the purposes for wider industry option of cloud computing technology." Another standards organization, the Unified Cloud Interface (UCI) was formed by CCIF and it aims to create a standard programmatic point of access to an entire cloud infrastructure. Additionally, in the Open Virtual Format (OVF) the aim is to pack and distribute software to be run on virtual machines so that virtual appliances can be made portable. Thus, efficient management of cloud service providers means efficient management of virtualized resource pools. The multi-dimensional nature of virtual machines complicates the process of finding a good mapping of virtual machines onto available physical hosts while maximizing user utility. Management of this data is also an issue.

17. Data centers also consume a huge amount of electricity. As per the report published by HP, "100 server racks can consume 1.3 MW of power and another 1.3 MW are required by the cooling system. This costs US dollars 2.6 million per year." Besides this monetary cost, data centers also impact the environment in terms of CO_2 emissions from cooling systems.

18. It is necessary to optimize application performance so that dynamic resource management can also improve utilization and thus reduce energy consumption in data centers. This can be achieved by consolidating workloads onto smaller numbers of servers and turning off idle resources.

1.15 ADVANTAGES AND DISADVANTAGES OF CLOUD COMPUTING

Let's first look at the advantages of cloud computing:

1. **Resource Management:** When you deploy your application and services to the cloud, the necessary virtual machines, network bandwidth, and other infrastructure resources are provided for you. If machines go down for hardware updates or because of unexpected failures, the cloud locates new virtual machines for your application automatically. Because you will *only pay for what you use*, you can start with a smaller investment. Doing so avoids incurring the typical upfront costs required for an on-premises deployment. This can be especially useful for smaller companies. In an on-premises scenario, small organizations might not have the data center space, IT skills, or hardware skills necessary to deploy their applications successfully. For example, the automatic infrastructure services that Microsoft Azure provides offer a low barrier for entry for application deployment and management.

2. **Dynamic Scaling:** The process of scaling out and scaling back your application depending on resource requirements is known as *dynamic scaling*. It is also known as *elastic scaling*. With cloud services, you create roles that work together to implement your application logic. For example, one web role could host the ASP.NET front end of your application. One or more worker roles could perform necessary background tasks. One or more virtual machines hosting each role are called *role instances*. Requests are load balanced across these instances. In this scenario, as resource demands increase, you can provision new role instances to handle the load. Furthermore, when demand decreases, you can remove these instances so that you do not have to pay for unnecessary computing power. There are also options for automatically

scaling up and down based on pre-defined rules and policies. This is very different from an on-premises deployment where you must over-provision hardware to anticipate peak demands if you want more control over automatic scaling than the platform provides. It is also possible to scale out websites and virtual machines. If your application requires fluctuating or unpredictable demands for computing resources, a cloud like MS Azure allows you to easily adjust your resource utilization to match the load.

3. **High Availability and Durability:** Cloud vendors like MS Azure provide a platform for applications that can reliably store and access server data through its storage services. Cloud applications like MS Azure have the MS Azure SQL Database for the same purpose. It ensures high availability of compute resources. For websites, you can meet the requirements of SLAs with only a single instance. For cloud services and virtual machines, you can meet the SLA requirements by having at least two instances per role or machine type. For virtual machines, the instances must be interchangeable and load balanced. It is the cloud vendor like MS Azure that monitors the actual hardware that hosts these virtual machines and instances. Furthermore, vendors like MS Azure are able to respond quickly to hardware restarts or failures by deploying new instances or moving application code and processing to other working hardware. The cloud vendors like Azure ensure high availability and durability for data stored by one on its storage services. MS Azure storage services replicate all data to at least three different servers. By default, this storage also replicates to a secondary MS Azure region. Similarly, MS Azure SQL Database replicates all data to guarantee availability and durability.

4. **Highly Available Services:** Say there is an online store that is deployed in MS Azure. Note that because this online store is a revenue generator, it is important and critical to keep it up and running. To achieve this objective, the Azure data center performs service monitoring and automatic instance management. The online store must also stay responsive to customer demand. The elastic scaling ability of MS Azure accomplishes this. During peak shopping times, new instances can come online to handle the increased usage. Additionally, the online store must not lose orders. Both MS Azure and the Azure SQL Database provide highly available and durable storage options to hold the order details and state throughout the order life cycle. For the highest level of availability,

you can deploy the same application to multiple MS Azure regions. Furthermore, it is possible to design a service that remains available even if an entire MS Azure region experiences a temporary failure. Doing this requires proper synchronization architecture and procedures for routing users.

5. **Periodic Workloads:** These workloads include some applications like a demo or a utility application that you want to make available for only several days or weeks. They do not have to be run continuously. MS Azure allows you to easily create, deploy, and share that application. Once this purpose is achieved, you can remove the application and you are charged only for the time it was deployed.

   Case Study: Consider a big company that runs complex data analysis of sales numbers at the end of each month. Although processing intensive, the total time required to complete the analysis is at most two days. In an on-premises scenario, the server required for this work would be underutilized for the majority of the month. In MS Azure, the business would pay only for the time the analysis application is running in the cloud. Assume that the application architecture is designed for parallel processing. The scale out features of MS Azure would allow the company to create large numbers of worker role instances or virtual machines. By working together, these can complete work that is more complex in less time. In this case study, you should use code or scripting to automatically deploy the application at the appropriate time every month.

NOTE
When not in use, remove the deployment because this will avoid charges for compute time because just suspending the application is insufficient.

6. **Unpredictable Growth:** All businesses have a goal of rapid and sustainable growth. However, growth is not easy to achieve if a traditional on-premises model is used. If you do not meet the expected growth even after a large expenditure, then it means you have spent money on maintaining underutilized hardware and infrastructure. However, if growth happens more quickly than expected, you might be unable to handle the load. This results in lost business and poor customer experience. For smaller companies, there might not even be enough initial capital to prepare for or keep up with rapid growth. For example,

say there is a small sports news portal (specialized part of a website) that makes money from advertising. Here, the amount of revenue is directly proportional to the amount of traffic that the site generates. In this case, the initial capital for the venture is limited. Furthermore, the company does not have the money required to set up and run its own data center. However, by designing the website to run on MS Azure, the company can easily deploy its solution as an ASP.NET application. The application will use the MS Azure SQL Database for relational data and blob storage for pictures and videos. If the popularity of the website grows dramatically, the company can increase the number of web role instances for its front end. The company can also increase the size of the Azure SQL Database service. The blob storage has built-in scalability features within MS Azure. If business decreases, the company can remove any unnecessary instances. Because its revenue is proportional to the traffic on the site, MS Azure helps the company to start small, grow fast, and reduce risk. If you use MS Azure in your company, then you have full control to find out how you can manage your computing costs. You can decide to implement automatic scaling through the use of the Autoscale feature or through the use the Autoscaling Application Block. This can add or remove instances based on custom rules (pre-determined amount). For example, you might have 8 instances during business hours and 4 instances during non-business hours. You can also keep the number of instances constant and only increase them manually through the web portal as demand increases over time. MS Azure provides you with the flexibility to make the decisions that are right for your business.

7. **Workload Spikes:** This workload pattern also works on the principle of elastic scale, as explained earlier. Consider the example of a sports news portal once again. Now, even because its business is steadily growing, there is still the possibility of temporary spikes or bursts of activity. For example, assume that another popular news outlet refers to the site. This means that the number of visitors to the site could dramatically increase in a single day.

   Example 2: Consider a service that processes daily reports at the end of the day. When the business day closes, each office sends in a report that the company headquarters processes. Because the process is only active a few hours each day, it is also a candidate for elastic scaling and deployment. MS Azure is suitable for temporarily scaling out an application to handle load spikes and then scaling back after the event has passed.

8. **Infrastructure Offloading:** It has been observed that most cloud scenarios make use of the elastic scaling capability of MS Azure. Even applications that show steady workload patterns will achieve a significant cost savings using MS Azure cloud services. It is difficult and more expensive to manage your own data center because it is costlier in terms of energy, people, skills, hardware, software licensing, and facilities. Furthermore, it is difficult to understand how costs are tied to individual applications. MS Azure, however, brings those costs to minimum and allows more transparency as well.

   For example, MS Azure Virtual Machines (VM) and Virtual Network (VN) provide an easier method for migrating on-premises servers and networks to the cloud. However, transitioning on-premises applications to cloud services or websites also alleviates the pressure on the on-premises data center. MS Azure and not these data centers are actually responsible for providing the required computing and storage resources for those applications. MS Azure also provides a pricing calculator for understanding specific costs. It also provides a Total Cost Of Ownership (TCO) calculator for estimating the overall cost reduction that a cloud incurs by adopting MS Azure.

9. Resource management, dynamic scaling, and high availability and durability are some of the main advantages of running applications in the cloud.

10. To ensure the highest levels of availability, for managing unpredictable growth and for handling workload spikes, MS Azure is preferred.

11. Quick service, safe and secure service, multiple user access, a development environment, and unlimited storage are some of its benefits.

12. Fewer operational issues, more reliability, more flexibility, innovation, and easier communication among teams and customers are real advantages.

Let's now look at the disadvantages of cloud computing:

1. Cloud services are more complex than traditional services.

2. Cloud-based software may not be a silver bullet for customers using it or companies who are deploying it.

3. A company that uses the cloud and its services will certainly rely on technology. Thus, the cloud is technology-based technology and if the technology fails somewhere, then the cloud will also fail.

4. Data on the cloud is quite insecure and needs to be tested extensively.

5. Since data on the cloud is redundant, there is a need for a redundancy tool.

6. There is no physical backup.

7. On the one hand, the cloud has increased business opportunities, while on the other hand it has disrupted several well-established IT businesses.

8. Transitions to cloud services must be cautious and calculated.

9. For critical applications, factors like data security, compliance, availability, and performance must also be considered.

10. Standards for cloud deployments are still in their infancy stage. This makes portability from one provider to another quite complex and unpredictable.

11. The cloud environment itself requires a strong foundation of best practices in software development, software architecture, and service management foundations.

12. The cloud uses data centers that consume large amounts of electricity. As per the HP report, 100 server racks can consume 1.3MW of power and another 1.3MW are required by the cooling system. This costs $2.6 million per year. These data centers impact the environment in terms of CO_2 emissions from the cooling systems. Thus, it is necessary to minimize energy consumption in data centers.

1.16 CLOUD COMPUTING APPLICATIONS

Cloud computing has several applications in IT today. Some of them are as follows:

1. The cloud can be used with web and mobile applications easily because these applications are easily scalable.

2. Cloud testing can be done using constantly configured resources, lower expenditure, and fewer release cycles.

3. Gaming applications can be easily implemented in the cloud.

4. ECG analysis can easily be done in the cloud.

5. Studying protein structures.

6. Satellite image processing.

7. The cloud takes CRM and ERP to the next level.

8. Social networking is very common nowadays. Thus, social cloud architecture is now available in the literature. In the social cloud, services can be mapped to particular users through Facebook identification.

SUMMARY

Cloud computing has deep ramifications in almost every field now. Cloud engineering is not far away either. Cloud analysis, cloud design, cloud coding, cloud testing, and cloud maintenance are all current hotspot research areas of the cloud. Mobile cloud computing, cloud security, and cloud energy efficiency are some of the potential areas of research today. Research into the field of cloud computing has changed the way IT services are invented, developed, scaled, and maintained. *Information* and *services* can be programmatically aggregated. Both act as the building blocks of complex compositions called *service mashups*. Many service providers such as Amazon, Facebook, and Google have made their service APIs public by using standard protocols like SOAP and REST. Thus, fully functional web applications can be developed easily just by gluing pieces together with a few LOC (Lines of Code).

CONCEPTUAL SHORT QUESTIONS WITH ANSWERS

Q1. What is the definition of a duty cycle in cloud computing?

Ans. 1 As we know, cloud data centers have several servers. This increases energy consumption. These servers are designed to be overloaded and overdesigned for better reliability. They must support redundancy, error-correcting RAM, parity disk drives, (n + 1) power supplies, et cetera. These devices need energy to cool and power them, light for the data center, security, and so on. This concept of purposely overdesigning a true server for a constant reliable operation is known as a *duty cycle*.

Q2. What is Eucalyptus?

Ans. 2 Eucalyptus is open source software that implements an Amazon Web Services compatible cloud, which is cost-effective, flexible, and secure. Eucalyptus is an acronym for Elastic Utility Computing Architecture for Linking Your Programs to Useful Systems. Its development started in 2003, at Rice University (TX) as a research project. In 2014, it was acquired by HP. They had their own cloud offerings under the HPE Helion banner. Now both have been combined as HPE Helion Eucalyptus. It can be easily deployed in existing IT infrastructures to exploit the benefits of both public and private cloud models. Eucalyptus provides an Infrastructure as a Service (IaaS). The main benefit is that it provides easy and secure deployment. A private cloud is deployed on the premises of an enterprise. It can be accessed by the users over an intranet. Thus, vital data remains secure from outside intrusions. It also provides AWS APIs. Therefore, at any time, consumers can easily migrate or load balance their sensitive data onto the Amazon public cloud. They need not worry about the flexibility of their network.

Q3. Name some companies that offer cloud service development.

Ans. 3 Some of the companies offering cloud services are the following:

(a) Amazon

(b) Google App Engine

(c) IBM

(d) Salesforce.com

(e) MS Azure

Q4. Mention some cloud services development tools.

Ans. 4 Some of the cloud services development tools are the following:

(a) Mosso

(b) Nirvanix

(c) Skytap

(d) StrikeIron

(e) 3tera

(f) 10gen

(g) Cohesive Flexible Technologies

(h) Joyent

Q5. List some issues associated with the cloud.

Ans. 5 Some of the issues associated with the cloud are the following:

(a) Technical issues

(b) Business model issues

(c) Internet issues

(d) Security issues

(e) Compatibility issues

(f) Social issues

Q6. What is a blog?

Ans. 6 A blog is a personal journal put up on a net/web log. It focuses on one topic and does not require much formatting. It is simple to create. As each blog has its own URL, it is an easy way of adding new URLs, which increase a site's popularity with search engines. A blog is an ideal vehicle for advertising your business and its products. The syndication that is built into blog management means that the advertisement can reach a wide audience. Thus, the blog will attract visitors to your site who would not otherwise find it. If we use blogs as an e-marketing tool then they should be updated regularly.

To create a blog, go to *www.blogger.com*, which is owned by Google .

Q7. Using a clear diagram, show the cloud architecture.

Ans. 7 Cloud architecture can be shown as follows:

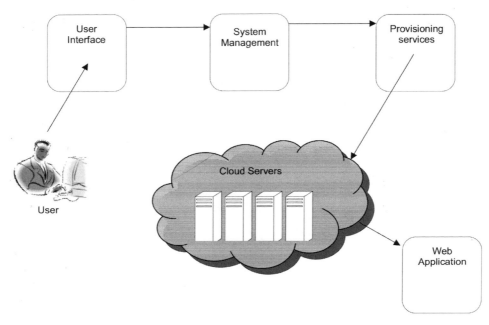

Q8. Explain the VMM (Virtual Machine Monitor) platform VMware ESXi.

Ans. 8 VMware is a company that provides a set of tools ranging from server and desktop virtualization to high-level management tools. ESXi is a VMM from VMware. A VMM or hypervisor mediates access to the physical hardware where it presents to each guest OS, a virtual machine (VM) that is a set of virtual platform interfaces. ESXi is a bare-metal hypervisor, that is, it installs directly on the physical server whereas others may require a host OS too. It provides advanced virtualization techniques for processor, memory, and I/O.

Q9. What is the basic concept behind virtualization?

Ans. 9 Using virtualization, one or more physical servers can be configured and partitioned into multiple independent virtual servers, all functioning independently and appearing to the user to be a single physical device. Such "virtual servers" do not physically exist and can therefore be moved around and scaled up or down on the fly without affecting the end user. Furthermore, the computing resources have now become "granular." This provides the end user and operator benefits including on-demand self-service, broad access across multiple devices, resource pooling, rapid elasticity, and service metering capability. An individual user who has permission to access the server can use the server's processing power to run an application, store data, or perform any other computing task. Therefore, instead of using a PC every time to run an application, the individual can now run the application from anywhere in the world, because the server provides the processing power to the application and the server is also connected to a network via the Internet or other connection platforms to be accessed from anywhere. This has become possible due to the increased computer processing power now available.

Q10. What is MS Azure?

Ans. 10 Previously it was known as Windows Azure and now it is called *Microsoft Azure*. It was released on February 1, 2010. It is a cloud computing platform and infrastructure for building, deploying, and managing applications and services through a global network of Microsoft-managed data centers. It provides both PaaS and IaaS services and supports many different programming languages, tools, and frameworks. Azure is an Internet-scale computing and services platform hosted in data centers managed or supported by Microsoft.

Q11. What are cloud data centers? Give examples.

Ans. 11 Cloud data centers are huge. Many have hundreds of thousands of square feet of space. MS highlights the fact that *one of its Azure data centers takes up as much space as ten football fields*. Clouds are expensive. Many cloud regions are actually comprised of two or more distinct data centers. Cloud data centers are showing up in clusters around major Internet hubs. In a nutshell, cloud providers have under-invested in emerging markets with high Internet use. Note that some data center regions have servers grouped inside containers, each containing 1800–2500 servers. The locations of data centers are in the North Central United States, Chicago (North America), South America's Brazil, China, Hong Kong, Singapore, North and Western Europe, Japan, and Australia.

NOTE   *CDN nodes are located in 24 countries.*

Q12. Define dynamic scaling.

Ans. 12 This refers to the capability to both scale out and scale back your application depending on resource requirements. It is also called an *elastic scale*.

Q13. Distinguish between horizontal and vertical scaling.

Ans. 13 The process of combining several independent computers as one to offer more processing power is known as *horizontal scaling*. This type of scaling implies several instances of an operating system existing on individual servers. On the other hand, the process of adding resources like storage, processors, and so on, to expand the processing capability is known as *vertical scaling*. This type of scaling makes use of a single instance of an OS.

Q14. Cloud computing architecture consists of a front end and a back end. Explain.

Ans. 14 The front end is the side that the client sees and the back end is the cloud section of a system. However, a cloud infrastructure consists of storage, a network, and computing components.

CHAPTER REVIEW QUESTIONS

Q1. Define cloud computing. Discuss its benefits, challenges, issues, and characteristics.

Q2. Distinguish between public and private clouds.

Q3. Explain different cloud models with examples.

Q4. Define the following terms related to the cloud:
  (a) Elasticity
  (b) Capacity planning
  (c) Horizontal and vertical scaling

Q5. What is MTBF? When is MTBF high?

[Hint: If a system needs long-lived nodes in a cloud infrastructure then the Mean Time Between Failures (MTBF) of a virtual server is less than that for the underlying hardware. It is governed by the number of physical nodes. The MTBF is higher for a given node when there are fewer physical nodes in the cloud-based transactional system. The overall MTBF helps to reduce the failure rate of the individual nodes.]

Q6. List some web-based presentation programs.

[Hint: Google Presentations, Preezo, and Zoho Show.]

Q7. Name six key properties of the cloud.

[Hint: User-centric, task-centric, powerful, accessible, intelligent, and programmable.]

Q8. Distinguish between the following:

(a) Public and community clouds

(b) Private and hybrid clouds

(c) Private and public clouds

Q9. Compare IAAS, PAAS, and SAAS with suitable examples.

Q10. Discuss some limitations of cloud computing.

Q11. What are data centers? Why are they needed?

Q12. Write a short summary of the evolution of cloud computing.

Q13. Define the following terms:

(a) Mashups

(b) Duty cycle

Q14. Is a grid a cloud? Is a cloud HPC (high-performance computing)?

Q15. The public cloud is like the Internet and a private cloud is like an intranet. Explain.

Q16. Write a short summary of MS Azure.

Q17. Why should a company shift to cloud computing?

Q18. What are cloud data centers (CDC)? Discuss some of the issues related to them.

Q19. What are workload spikes?

Q20. Explain cloud adoption in detail.

2

CLOUD COMPUTING ARCHITECTURES

2.1 INTRODUCTION

The elements and sub-elements needed for cloud computing represent the cloud computing architecture. These elements are the front-end platform, back-end platform, cloud-based delivery, and a network. They consist of cloud services, middleware, software components, resources, their geo-location, and their attributes. Organizations deploying the cloud must take all of these issues into account. The cloud architecture consists of a front end (client-side) and a back end (cloud section). *Front end* refers to the client devices that the user employs to access the cloud computing system. Different interfaces exist for different applications. For instance, email is a web service that uses existing web browsers like Google Chrome, Firefox, Mozilla, and so on. On the other hand, the back end involves the cloud itself. It consists of servers, computers, and data storage systems that are used by the users. Every application has its own server for services. A central server is established. The server follows some rules called *protocols*. It uses a special type of software, called *middleware,* to communicate with the users who are connected to the cloud server.

2.2 COMPONENTS OF CLOUDS—LOGICAL REFERENCE MODEL

The cloud computing reference model establishes a standardized process for modeling clouds. The Cloud Computing Reference Model (CCRM) consists of four supporting models as follows:

(a) **Cloud Enablement Model:** This is the core model of the CCRM. It explains the fundamental technology tiers of cloud computing capabilities provided by the cloud platform and cloud service providers to potential consumers of cloud-enabled technology.

(b) **Cloud Deployment Model:** This model describes the range of cloud deployment scenarios available to your enterprise—internal/private cloud, external/public cloud, hybrid/integrated cloud, and community or vertical cloud. These deployment scenarios may be mixed and matched.

(c) **Cloud Governance and Operations Model:** This model describes the governance, security operations, support, management, and monitoring requirements for cloud computing to ensure that you have considered all of the potential operational risks for adopting the cloud for your organization.

(d) **Cloud Ecosystem Model:** This model considers the requirements of developing and sustaining a cloud ecosystem comprised of cloud providers, cloud consumers, and cloud intermediaries, as well as the cloud network and *cloud dial tone* necessary to ensure that the cloud is always there for you. The cloud ecosystem also includes the various cloud enablement technologies and cloud providers and consumers of those cloud-enabled technologies that comprise the cloud ecosystem.

The cloud computing reference model is shown in Figure 2.1.

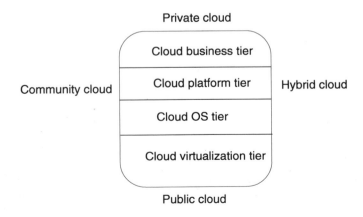

FIGURE 2.1 Cloud computing reference model.

The main components of the CCRF are as follows:

1. **Cloud Enablement Model:**
   - Cloud virtualization tier
   - Cloud operating system tier
   - Cloud platform tier
   - Cloud business tier

2. **Cloud Deployment Model:**
   - Internal/private cloud
   - External/public cloud
   - Hybrid/integrated cloud
   - Community/vertical/shared by a community with stakeholder interests

3. **Cloud Governance and Operations Model:**
   - Governance, culture, and behavior
   - Security and privacy
   - Management and monitoring
   - Operations and support

4. **Cloud Ecosystem Model:**
   - Cloud network/dial tone
   - Cloud ecosystem enablement
   - Cloud consumers and cloud providers
   - Cloud physical access, integration, and distribution

Logical Architecture Foundation

The logical architecture of the cloud first requires that we separate the layers of the cloud architecture. NIST provides us with a cloud reference architecture. According to NIST, it is a high-level model consisting of three tiers of cloud capabilities "as-a-service." NIST specifies that there are three categories of the cloud: infrastructure, platform, and software—all as a "service" architecture. Figure 2.2 shows the NIST architecture.

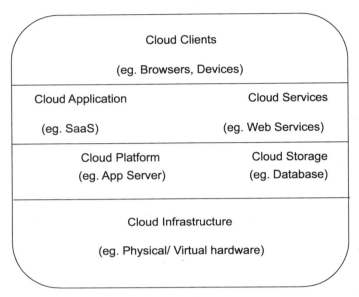

FIGURE 2.2 Six-tier logical cloud stack.

Figure 2.2, explicitly defines and identifies cloud services.

From Figures 2.1 and 2.2, it is easier to see the different tiers of the cloud.

1. **Cloud Physical Tier:** This tier provides the physical computing, storage, network, and security resources that are virtualized and cloud enabled to support cloud requirements. It is important to understand that this physical tier provides the substrate on which cloud virtualization technologies and cloud operating system platforms are built to enable higher-order cloud patterns to be realized.

2. **Cloud Virtualization Tier:** This tier provides core physical hardware virtualization and provides a potentially useful foundation for cloud computing.

3. **Cloud Operating System Tier:** This tier provides the cloud computing "fabric" as well as application virtualization, core cloud provisioning, metering, billing, load balancing, workflow, and related functionality

typical of cloud platforms. This tier is represented by a wide variety of new cloud platforms and cloud enablement technologies.

4. **Cloud Platform Tier:** This tier provides technical solutions, application and messaging middleware, application servers, and so on, that comprise cloud and/or application platforms as well as pre-integrated cloud and application platforms themselves, offered via PaaS delivery models.

5. **Cloud Business Tier:** This tier comprises the business or mission exploitation of cloud-enabled business applications, software, data, content, knowledge, and the associated analysis frameworks and other cloud consumption models that facilitate and enable end user business value from the cloud consumer's ability to access, bind, and consume cloud capabilities.

CCRM follows some rules and guidelines.

1. Cloud tiers enable higher-level tiers.

2. Each cloud tier, working from the bottom up in the CCRM enables the cloud tier above it.

3. These tiers build upon one another but yet they are independent.

4. Cloud tiers are individually *atomic* and individually accessible.

5. Cloud consumers can access and consume cloud-enabled resources directly from any of these tiers, independent of the others via cloud Application Programming Interfaces (APIs) and a portal or a self-service user interface of some fashion.

6. The cloud enablement tiers help to organize various classes of cloud-enabled resources into the CCRM.

7. Note that cloud consumers do not access these tiers directly but rather use cloud-enabled resources.

8. Each cloud tier must have the necessary cloud network/dial tone and cloud ecosystem enablement capabilities in order to be discoverable, provisionable, and consumable as a service via the cloud.

9. Cloud providers and consumers must be able to find one another, communicate and negotiate, and then engage by establishing business and technical relationships via a service contract and better technical interfaces to cloud capabilities, with clear SLAs and QoS.

2.3 TYPES OF CLOUDS

Users control cloud computing using networked client devices, such as PCs, laptops, tablets, and smartphones. Three types of clouds are defined in the literature and they are described below.

1. **Private Cloud:** This type is a cloud infrastructure operated solely for a single organization, which is either managed internally or by a third-party, or hosted internally or externally. Self-run data centers are generally capital intensive. They have a significant footprint, requiring allocations of space, hardware, and environmental controls. These assets have to be refreshed periodically, resulting in additional capital expenditures.

2. **Public Clouds:** A cloud is said to be public when the services are rendered over a network that is open for public use. Technically speaking, there may be no or little difference between public and private cloud architectures, but security may be different for services that are made available by a service provider for a public audience and when communication is effected over a non-trusted network. In general, public cloud service providers like Amazon AWS, Microsoft, and Google own and operate the infrastructure and offer access only via the Internet, that is, no direct connectivity is offered.

3. **Hybrid Cloud:** This type is a combination of two or more clouds (private, public, or community) that remain distinct entities, but are bound together, offering the benefits of multiple deployment models. Note that hybrid can also mean the ability to connect collocation, managed, and/or dedicated services with cloud resources. Different use cases for hybrid cloud combinations exist.

   Example 1: An organization may store sensitive client data in-house on a private cloud application but interconnect that application to a billing application provided on a public cloud as a service. Thus, here the hybrid cloud extends the capabilities of the enterprise to deliver a specific business service through the addition of externally available public cloud services.

   Example 2: In this case, an organization uses public cloud computing resources to meet temporary capacity needs that cannot be met by the private cloud. This capability enables hybrid clouds to employ cloud bursting for scaling across clouds. Cloud bursting is an application deployment model in which an application runs in a private cloud or data center and "bursts" to a public cloud when demand for computing capacity increases. In addition, the primary advantage of cloud bursting and a hybrid cloud model is that an organization only pays for extra compute resources when they are needed.

2.4 CLOUD DBMS (CDBMS)—CLUSTERING AND REPLICATION

Cloud Database Management Systems (CDBMSs) are defined as distributed databases that provide computing as a service but not a product. The challenge is to manage persistent data. The challenge is bigger now because database servers existing in the cloud are less reliable (can fail easily). When this happens then files related to DBMS may also become corrupted. However, it is easier to recover a server from a failure in a virtualized environment than in a physical environment. This is because the database administrator can simply replace the corrupt image with a new instance from the database machine image. Two techniques may be used here:

(a) Clustering

(b) Replication

Let's define these techniques.

Clustering: This is a technique where multiple (many) database servers will work together as a single logical database server in a clustered database environment. It is very complex and also more costly. It requires an expert database administrator (DBA). The advantage here is that the database clients do not know when a node fails and they can continue operating. It depends on the clusters. It is important to note that the more complex the clustering is, the more potential points of failure there will be. Even if there is dynamic assignment of IP addresses within the cloud, new issues will arise.

Replication: This technique is where the database is replicated and it contains a main server known as a *database master*. It is an alternative to the clustering technique. A single database server, the database master, replicates the data to one or more database slaves. The client applications performs write transactions to the database master. The transactions that become successful are then reflected to the database servers. The advantage here is that it is easy to implement replication without also requiring a large numbers of servers. However, clustering is more reliable than the replication method. This is because with the replication method, if the master-database fails then the slave-database cannot work until the master recovers from the failure. This is not the case for clustering.

2.5 SERVICE MODELS

Three types of cloud computing services exist in the industry. The term *services* means reusing components (every resource) across a provider's network. In SaaS, the software is available for a service. This implies that you can use the software but do not own it. In PaaS, the developer is the owner of the application and the data. In IaaS, the administrator chooses and manages the activities from the operating system onward, but has no control over the machines. In summary:

- Software is available for the service (in SaaS)—you use the software but do not own it.

- Platform is available for the service (in PaaS)—you use the platform to develop web applications.

- Hardware and software is available for the service (in IaaS)—you use the hardware and software as a VM.

- These service models are described in detail in the following section.

2.5.1 SaaS (Software-as-a-Service)/Application-as-a-Service (AaaS)

Application-as-a-Service (AaaS) or SaaS is defined as a software model in which both the application and the relevant data is hosted on a cloud by independent developers, which enables a user to access the software as and when required from any location. Examples include email sites, social media sites, and so on.

We would even consider Microsoft Business Productivity Online Suite (BPOS) and Dynamics CRM Online to be some examples of SaaS.

SaaS is a software delivery business model where a provider or third party hosts an application and makes it available to customers on a subscription basis. SaaS customers use the software running on the provider's infrastructure on a pay-as-you-go basis. Customers do not have to commit to any long-term contracts. Depending on the contract, customers can quit using the software at any time. It is important to understand that in SaaS, the underlying infrastructure and the software configuration are invisible to the users. Thus, the users have to settle for the functionality that is provided. In addition, SaaS uses a highly multi-tenant architecture and the user contexts are separated from one another logically at both runtime and rest. Collaboration applications that solve the same problem across many enterprises have been very successful in the SaaS arena. Remember that because the hardware and software configuration is transparent to the end users, there is minimal if any need for professional IT involvement. Some SaaS applications can even be customized by the end users. The point is that SaaS empowers business units to bypass IT procurement processes. Enterprise architecture teams need to realize this aspect and teach these business units about the importance of governance. In addition, the teams should design new governance processes or modify the existing ones to accommodate SaaS.

The following points characterize SaaS/AaaS:

1. The customers rent software that is hosted by the vendor such as Microsoft or Amazon, and so on.

2. An Internet connection is required here.

3. This model is analogous to ASPs (Application Service Providers), wherein a provider hosts available applications/software for the users and delivers those over the web. Yet, there are some differences between these two models (Table 2.1). These differences are enumerated in the table.

TABLE 2.1 Comparison of ASP and SaaS

ASP	SaaS
1. ASP applications are usually single-tenant with client–server architecture hosted by a third party with HTML as a front end.	1. It is a multi-tenant application hosted by the application developer, with regular updates directly from the developer.
2. It may be a non-virtualized environment with direct storage capability.	2. It is shared. Virtualized servers, network, and storage systems are the main constituents of its resource pool.
3. It is not build to be web-based or on the Internet.	3. It is built to be web-based and used over the public Internet.

4. All customers can use the same software version.

5. Global accessibility and easier administration are some of its benefits.

6. Tasks like software deployment, software maintenance (changes), cloud software testing, patching, and so on, are all managed by the provider.

7. In a nutshell, SaaS is what a provider hosts as software (service) that is centrally located and that can be made easily available to customers via the Internet on a pay-per-use basis.

8. Thus, commercial software is accessible through the web.

9. APIs allow for integration between different pieces of software.

10. Security is a serious issue here because all the data is available in the cloud.

11. There is slow switching between different SaaS vendors.

12. Time critical applications, that is, applications that demand response time in milliseconds, are not benefited by SaaS.

13. Multi-tenancy means sharing of the resources by many users. SaaS has two modes—simple multi-tenancy and fine-grained multi-tenancy. In the simple multi-tenancy case, every user has their own resources, which are different from other users. On the other hand, in fine-grained multi-tenancy all resources are shared except customer-related data.

14. Web applications like blogs, social networks, web content management, and WIKI services are all applications of SaaS only.

15. Enterprise services like desktop software, workflow management, supply chain management, and CRM are all applications of SaaS only.

16. Clients are very much interested in moving their applications to SaaS platforms because they can reduce their monitoring of many servers.

17. In the SaaS cloud, the vendor supplies the hardware infrastructure, software, and applications. The customer interacts with the application through a portal.

18. Some SaaS providers include MS Live CRM, MS Azure, Google Apps, Trend Micro, Symantec, and Zoho.

19. Cloud applications have a global scope while SaaS has more of a centralized hosting platform.

20. SaaS is like a "thin app" where client machines need only a web browser with some sort of plug-in to provide additional functionality.

21. Applications reside on top of the cloud stack. Services are provided by this layer. These services can be accessed by the end users through web portals. Conventional applications like MS Word, MS Excel, and so on, are accessed as a service on the web in real time.

22. Salesforce.com relies on the SaaS model only. It offers business productivity applications that reside fully on their servers. Thus, customers can customize according to their needs in real time.

2.5.2 PaaS (Platform-as-a-Service)

In this model, the developer creates software using tools and the other utilities of a cloud provider. For example, websites are designed, developed, and hosted on the cloud. PaaS fills the needs of those who want to build and run custom applications as services. These could be ISVs, value-added service providers, or enterprise IT shops. PaaS offers hosted application servers that have near-finite scalability owing to their reliance on large resource pools. PaaS also offers the necessary supporting services such as storage, security, integration, infrastructure, and development tools for a complete platform. A service provider offers a pre-configured, virtualized application server environment to which applications can be deployed by the development staff. Since the service providers manage the hardware (patching, upgrades etc.,) as well as the application server uptime, the involvement of IT professionals is minimized. It is important to understand that PaaS is suitable for brand-new applications, as legacy applications often require extensive refactoring to comply with sandbox rules.

Case Study on AccuWeather

Consider a case study of the AccuWeather company. This company provides weather forecasts. It needed better solutions to handle more than 4 billion daily data requests. To increase scalability, the company began delivering content from the cloud on the Windows Azure platform. As a result, the company could bring in the downtime required for development and proofs of concept without worrying about provisional infrastructure. It also gained on-demand scalability, improved access to real-time weather data, and cut IT costs by up to 40%. The vice president of the company stated, "With MS Azure we gained velocity because we can be innovative without worrying about complex infrastructure. A proof of concept that might have taken three months to execute now takes three days."

The following points characterize PaaS as a service:

1. It provides hardware, OS, storage, and network capacity on a pay-per-use basis via Internet only.

2. It provides services for application development and deployment.

3. It allows users to create web applications rapidly. There is no overhead for the cost and complexity of buying and hardware/software management.

4. It is used to build multi-tenant applications, that is, services that can be accessed by multiple users simultaneously.

5. The applications can be deployed on the cloud using tools and different programming languages supported by a particular provider. The web developer will simply write the code using PaaS services. It is the job of the PaaS provider to upload that code and make it online available through the Internet.

6. There is more security because customer environments are separated from each other.

7. An Internet connection is required.

8. Google App Engine (GAE), LongJump, Force.com, WaveMaker, MS Azure, and CloudBees are some of the PaaS providers.

9. The main aim of the GAE is to run the user's web application efficiently. It maintains Java-Runtime-Environments (JRE) and Python on the application servers. It includes simple APIs to access Google services. Now applications are able to integrate data services and other GAE services like email, image storage, and so on.

10. MS Azure offers a service called *SQL Azure* that stores data in the cloud.

11. When looking for a PaaS provider, the basic goal should be reduced time-to-market and not cost savings. Other factors like high availability, security, and scalability are also vital for developers and cloud testers.

12. A good PaaS environment should support caching for cloud resources because it increases performance. This functionality needs APIs to put an object or a resource in the cache.

13. The PaaS environment must have a browser-based development studio with an IDE for development, test, and debugging of applications.

14. It must support very secure and on-demand collaboration throughout the SDLC.

15. Hadoop software enables applications to work easily with thousands of nodes and petabytes of data and is based on Java. PaaS must be able to monitor such operations.

2.5.3 IaaS (Infrastructure-as-a-Service)/HaaS (Hardware-as-a-Service)

IaaS is a model where the cloud provides both hardware and software. IaaS can be compared to the creation of Virtual Machines (VM) on the cloud infrastructure. With VMs one can launch Windows Server, MS SQL Server, Oracle, MangoDB, SharePoint Server, and Linux in minutes and then scale up from one to thousands of VM instances. VMs can be used on-demand to get a scalable compute infrastructure when you need flexible resources. It is also possible to create VMs that run Windows, Linux, and enterprise applications or capture your own images to create custom VMs. IaaS is analogous to traditional hosting where a business will use the hosted environment as a logical extension of the on-premises data center. Note that the servers (physical and virtual) are rented on an as-needed basis and the IT professionals who manage the infrastructure have full control of the software configuration. In addition, some providers may even allow flexibility in the hardware configuration, which makes the service more expensive when compared to an equivalent PaaS offering. The development staff will build, test, and deploy applications with full awareness of the hardware and software configuration of the servers.

For instance, customers like Webzeb, Telenor, Avanade, Toyota, and so on, are using VMs over the MS Azure platform.

Case Study on Telenor

Using MS Azure-based VMs, the Telenor company has dramatically reduced the costs needed for test, development, and demo environments, reduced the time to make the environments available to the project, and saved on long-term investments in hardware that would have only needed to be used in the short term.

Case Study on Toyota

Toyota is a company that has 16 websites that deliver more than 100 million page views per month. To enhance site content, increase scalability, and reduce the cost of ownership, Toyota is rebuilding the site using the MS Azure cloud development environment.

The following points characterize Iaas/HaaS:

1. It is a virtual provider of computing resources such as hardware, storage services, devices, networking, operating systems, virtualization technology, and so on.

2. This service provider owns the required equipment and is responsible for configuring, running, and maintaining it.

3. It is defined as a process for making available cloud computing infrastructure resources, that is, servers, storage, network, and operating systems as an on-demand service. Rather than purchasing servers, software, data center space, or network items, clients instead buy those resources as a fully outsourced service on demand.

4. Amazon Web Services (AWS) is an IaaS provider.

5. IaaS can be considered a basic template for other services in the cloud like SaaS and PaaS.

6. IaaS providers will act promptly when there is a need to scale up or down and this is known as *autoscaling*.

7. It provides elastic load balancing that auto-distributes the incoming traffic related to an application to different instances of virtual computers. Thus, elasticity is also possible.

8. It is a platform independent service.

9. It charges only for the resources that are used.

10. It also supports a multi-tenant architecture, which represents several users who can work on a single piece of hardware.

11. Scaling of resources can be done as needed.

12. Its scalability is therefore flexible.

13. No need for hardware administration and maintenance.

14. Location independence is another feature because users can access the service from anywhere with an Internet connection.

15. Because cloud hosts are redundant, if one network or server fails then there is no effect on the data centers due to multiple hardware resources. In the worst case scenario, if the entire data center fails, then there would be secondary and tertiary data centers for smooth functioning.

16. Less risk in Return On Investment (ROI).

17. IaaS comprises two types:

    (a) **Computation as a service:** Here, VM servers are charged per hour. It depends on the VM capacity including RAM size and CPU, OS, and the features of that VM.

    (b) **Data as a service:** In this type of IaaS, there is no restriction on storage space to store the data related to the user. Charging is done on a per GB basis for data transfer.

18. *InstaCompute* is an example of an IaaS provider by Tata communications that is cost-effective, flexible, and reliable. It offers variable computing power that can meet different business needs as per requirements. It allows removal of virtual servers, metered Internet connectivity, storage capacity, and dynamic additions. It is secure, uses a pay-per-use model, and assures service levels per business requirements.

19. IaaS clouds can even be one of three types: private IaaS clouds, public IaaS clouds, and hybrid IaaS clouds.

20. Companies such as Amazon EC2, Bluelock, and GoGrid offer IaaS. Amazon EC2 is a web service that offers dynamic scaling of computing capacity in the cloud. Bluelock offers cloud services supported by VMware cloud data center services. These data centers are very secure and also SAS-70 Type-II certified. GoGrid offers customers a user-friendly web service interface.

21. IaaS providers offer template OS images for virtual servers.

22. IaaS providers also have APIs to add, start, stop, access, configure, and delete the virtual host machine and storage.

2.6 DEPLOYMENT MODELS

There are three types of clouds: public, private, and hybrid clouds. However, several other clouds also exist and are discussed in this section.

2.6.1 Public Cloud/External Cloud

A cloud is said to be public/external when the services are rendered over a network that is open for public use. Technically speaking, there may be no or little difference between public and private cloud architecture but security may be different for services that are made available by a service provider for a public audience and when communication is carried out over a non-trusted network. In general, public cloud service providers like Amazon AWS, Microsoft, and Google own and operate the infrastructure and offer access only via the Internet, that is, no direct connectivity is offered.

In general, public clouds offer services over the Internet and are owned and operated by a cloud provider. For example, email services and social networking sites are all aimed at the general public. The following points characterize public clouds (or external clouds):

1. They offer services to users on the principle of pay-by-use (explained earlier).

2. They are run by third parties because they need a huge investment to build.

3. In this model, applications from different customers are mixed together on storage systems, cloud servers, and other infrastructures within the cloud.

4. The customers can choose a location to deploy the application. This mitigates latency, risks, time, and costs for the users.

5. Data control and security are important tasks here.

6. A public cloud is always larger than an organization's private cloud because it provides the ability to scale up, scale down, and to transfer the risks of an infrastructure from an organization to the cloud provider.

7. A public cloud is a better choice if the standardized workload for an application is used by several people, or you need to test and develop

application code or if you have SaaS applications from a cloud vendor. In addition, it may be a good choice if you need incremental capacity, that is, adding compute capacity at peak times, or if you are using collaboration projects or even if you are performing an ad hoc software development.

8. In this type of cloud, the service providers charge the companies according to their usage.

9. It is important to understand that here resources are owned or hosted by the cloud service providers (company) and the services are sold to other companies. This is shown in Figure 2.3.

10. No direct connectivity is provided by public cloud service providers like Amazon AWS, MS, and Google.

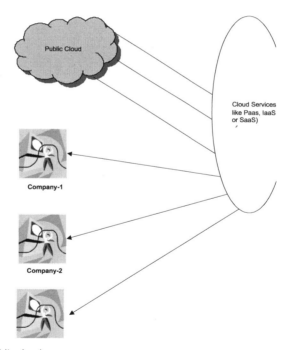

FIGURE 2.3 The public cloud.

2.6.2 Private Cloud

Just as the public cloud can be thought of as the Internet, similarly a private cloud can be thought of as an intranet. The following points characterize private or internal clouds:

1. A private cloud or internal cloud is used when the data center for the cloud is to be operated for a specific business only.

2. It serves the client with maximum security, quality of service, and data control.

3. The infrastructure is owned by the company and it has power over how applications are deployed on it.

4. With private clouds, the IT infrastructure of organizations can be merged. This mitigates electricity expenses as well.

5. These clouds are limited to the organizational boundary.

6. They can be set up from MS, IBM, VMware, Eucalyptus, OpenStack, and so on.

7. They are to be used when the security of your organization is of paramount importance.

8. Your company has sufficient potential, in terms of money, that it can run even a next-generation cloud data center most efficiently and effectively.

9. The cloud computing infrastructure that is designed only for a single company cannot be shared with other organizations.

10. These clouds are more costly and more secure.

11. The main objective of a private cloud is not to sell the cloud services to external organizations but to reap the benefits of the cloud architecture by securing the rights to manage your own data center.

12. Private clouds are virtual distributed systems that depend on private infrastructure only.

13. They provide internal users with dynamic provisioning of computing resources.

14. Therefore, security concerns are less critical here.

15. Testing a private cloud is cheaper than testing a public cloud.

16. The problem is that private clouds cannot scale up easily in case of heavy (peak) demands.

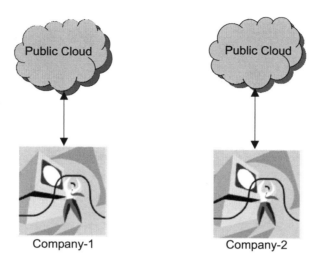

FIGURE 2.4 Private clouds.

To cope with all these problems, the only solution is to combine both public and private clouds to achieve a hybrid cloud.

The differences between public and private clouds are enumerated in Table 2.2. Hybrid clouds are discussed in the following section.

TABLE 2.2 Differences between Public and Private Clouds

Public Cloud	Private Cloud
1. Its owner is the cloud provider or third party.	1. Its owner is an organization only.
2. It involves fewer costs.	2. It involves higher costs.
3. Scalability is on demand and unlimited.	3. Scalability is limited to the infrastructure installed.
4. Less security.	4. More security.
5. Testing it is difficult because everything is public.	5. Testing is easier because it is a private cloud.
6. Performance is harder to obtain.	6. Performance is guaranteed.
7. Less management and control is needed because it works on the concept of virtualization.	7. More management and control is needed because it has a higher level of control over resources.

A private cloud is a cloud infrastructure operated solely for one organization, which is managed either internally or by a third-party and hosted internally or externally. Self-run data centers are generally capital intensive. They have a significant footprint, requiring allocations of space, hardware, and environmental controls. These assets have to be refreshed periodically, resulting in additional capital expenditures.

2.6.3 Hybrid Cloud

Because the focus has been to make the cloud more secure and yet to provide the same services and resource sharing, cloud infrastructures have naturally evolved to what is known as a *hybrid cloud.* Hybrid/mixed clouds can be explained with the help of an equation:

$$\text{Hybrid Cloud} = \text{Public Cloud} + \text{Private Cloud}$$

This means that now you can have the benefits of both internal network storage as well as a public data cloud that can be accessed from anywhere in the world using the Internet. Using broadband services along with the cloud, companies can connect to larger networks to make use of available resources. There is no need for a huge computer to handle complex tasks like database indexing.

The following points characterize hybrid clouds:

1. Better scalability and reliability because they allow companies to move from public to private clouds.

2. Better sharing of resources on demand.

3. They allow an approach for extending the infrastructure beyond the organizational firewall with more security.

4. More important applications are stored on hybrid clouds and less important applications and data are stored on a public cloud.

5. An example of hybrid usage would be something like a patient's record or some financial matters that cannot be put on public cloud servers because they are sensitive information. These services can make use of hybrid clouds.

6. This type of cloud is used during cloud bursting. In this case, an organization generally uses its own computing infrastructure but in case of higher load requirements, the company can access clouds. It is

important to understand that this means that a company using a hybrid cloud can manage an internal cloud/private cloud for its general usage and it can migrate the entire application to the public cloud during heavy peak hours.

7. This is shown as a diagram in Figure 2.4.

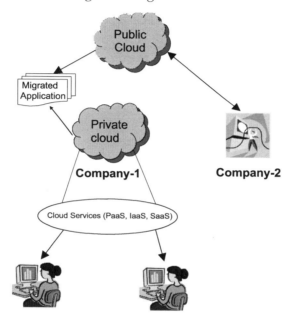

FIGURE 2.5 Hybrid clouds.

8. The purpose is to lease public cloud services when private cloud capacity is insufficient.

9. Sotomayor et al. states, "a hybrid cloud takes shape when a private cloud is supplemented with computing capacity from public clouds. And this method of temporarily renting a capacity to handle spikes in load is known as cloud bursting."

10. We can combine a private cloud with a public cloud or even a public one with community clouds.

11. Public clouds and community clouds are compared in Table 2.3

TABLE 2.3 Public Cloud versus Community Cloud

Public Cloud	Community Cloud
1. Any user who signs up can use a public cloud.	1. Only users within a particular industry segment/group can use it. These users have common objectives.
2. It uses a pay-per-use model, which is expensive.	2. It is more expensive because the site is customized for use by the company group.
3. There is less security.	3. It is more secure because a limited number of users have accounts.
4. The provider is not known to the consumer.	4. The provider is not known to the consumer.
5. Compliance with the regulations of an organization is not an objective.	5. The objective is to comply with the regulations of an organization.

12. Similarly, we can compare a private cloud and a hybrid cloud (Table 2.4).

TABLE 2.4 Private Cloud versus Hybrid Cloud

Private Cloud	Hybrid Cloud
1. It is fully set up by a company.	1. It uses the resources of a public provider on a pay-per-use model.
2. Performance is limited.	2. More scalable and elastic because it can use public resources to meet load spikes.
3. Less flexible.	3. More flexible because it can develop and test services on a public cloud and later deploy them on a private cloud.
4. It costs more.	4. It is cheaper.

2.6.4 Community Cloud

A community cloud is a type or variant of a private cloud but it goes beyond a business or an organization. It is implemented when several businesses have similar requirements and perspectives to share. They are accessible to other members of a particular community but are not available to the general public. Examples include branches of educational organizations and government, military, and industry suppliers.

The following points characterize community clouds:

1. They are needed when there is a necessity for general services.

2. By creating virtual machines from the machines that are underutilized, a community cloud can be established (Figure 2.3).

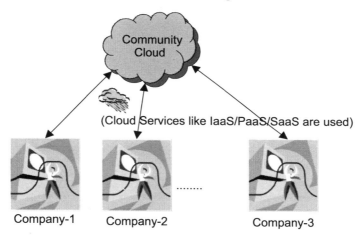

FIGURE 2.6 Community cloud.

2.6.5 Throwaway Clouds

In New York, another type of cloud was used wherein the cloud was rented for a short-term or a one-time project. This is similar to a situation where you are renting a car from an agency and returning it. This scenario means a lower cost per day. Clouds can be very similar to this model. For example, you can negotiate a portion of the SAP for a test drive and drop it into the cloud for the 99-day test drive.

The same concept can also be extended to VMware. Imagine a new car lot that is open 24/7 with thousands of different types of models and you can rent them. The point is that you do not have to struggle to set up an environment just for a test drive when the trial period is also short. Similarly in VMware systems, you just need to drop into a cloud or a VMware system and turn it ON. In addition, everything is configured and ready for you to explore. Such clouds are throwaway clouds.

2.6.6 Traveling Clouds

In 2007, MS Unified Communications Inc., tried to show their latest wares to *InfoWorld* editors. Assume that the entire constellation of servers for this scenario required 8 Windows servers, with one server requiring a 128-bit operating system. This was quite large. In such a case, the product manager hopped on a plane with a big USB hard drive and was engaged in preconfiguring the MS Unified Communications' constellation having an active server directory, SQL server for repository, file server, and so on. All the manager had to do was just change a single IP address on the exchange server for external connectivity. This is an example of a traveling cloud.

2.7 CLOUD INTEROPERABILITY AND STANDARDS

Clouds need to be standardized in two fields—standardizing parts of the cloud such as workloads, authentication, and data access as well as the parts that need to work together. The Cloud Standards Coordination WIKI maintains a list of some of these projects. Table 2.5 lists some of the cloud standardization efforts made so far along with their URLs.

TABLE 2.5 Cloud Standardization Efforts

Project Name	URL	Focus
Cloud Audit	www.cloudaudit.org	Open, extensible, and secure interface, namespace, and methodology for cloud providers and their consumers.
Cloud Computing Interoperability Forum	www.riverbed.com	Common, agreed-on framework for cloud platforms to exchange information in a unified manner.
Cloud Security Alliance	www.cloudsecurity-alliance.org	Recommended practices for cloud computing security.
Cloud Standards Customer Council	www.cloudstandardscustomercouncil.org	Standards, security, and interoperability issues related to migration to the cloud.

Cloud Storage Initiative	www.snia.org/cloud	Adoption of cloud storage as a new delivery model (Data-Storage-as-a-Service). Initiative sponsored by the Storage Networking Industry Association (SNIA), the creator and promoter of the Cloud Data Management Interface (CDMI). SNIA includes members from Oracle, NetApp, and EMC.
Delta Cloud	www.incubator.apache.org/	Abstraction layer for dealing with differences among IaaS providers. API based on representational state transfer (REST). It has libraries for seven providers including Amazon EC2, Eucalyptus, and Rackspace.
Distributed Management Task Force (DMTF)	www.dmtf.org/standards/ cloud	Management interoperability for cloud systems, developer of the Open Virtualization Framework (OVF).
IEEE P2301, Guide for Cloud Portability and Interoperability Profiles	www.standards.ieee.org/ develop/project/2301.html	Standards-based options for application interfaces, portability interfaces, management interfaces, interoperability interfaces, file formats, and operation conventions.
IEEE P2302, Draft Standard for Intercloud Interoperability and Federation.	www.standards.ieee.org/ develop/project/2302.html	Protocols for exchanging data, programmatic queries, functions and governance for cloud sharing data or functions.
OASIS Identity in the Cloud (IDCloud)	www.oasis-open.org/com-mittees/tc_home.php?wg_ abb rev = id-cloud	Performs risk analysis on collected use cases, also develops guidelines for reducing vulnerabilities.
Open Cloud Computing Interface	www.occi-wg.org	REST-based interfaces for management of cloud resources such as computing, storage, and bandwidth.

Open Cloud Consortium	www.opencloudconsortium.org	Frameworks for interoperability between clouds and the operation of the Open Cloud Testbed.
Open Data Center Alliance	www.opendatacenteralliance.org	Unified customer vision for long-term data center requirements, developing usage models for cloud vendors.
OpenStack	www.openstack.org	Open source software for running private clouds, founded by Rackspace and NASA.
Standards Acceleration to Jumpstart Adoption of Cloud Computing	https://www.nist.gov/itl	Cloud standards are obtained by providing use cases that can be supported on cloud systems. Use cases should show a set of documented and public cloud system specifications.
The Open Group Cloud Work Group	https://collaboration.opengroup.org/cloudcomputing/	Other cloud standards organizations and this cloud work group together to tell enterprises how to implement cloud services in their companies.

2.8 CLOUD INTEROPERABILITY USE CASES

Cloud consumer and cloud provider interactions are illustrated with the help of use cases in reference to cloud computing. Companies such as NIST, OMG, DMTF, and so on, have developed standards for data portability, cloud interoperability, security, and management. They have developed use cases for cloud computing.

Role of NIST: NIST defines a set of 21 use cases. They are classified into three groups:

(a) Cloud management use cases

(b) Cloud interoperability use cases

(c) Cloud security use cases

Cloud Management Use Cases:

- Opening an account
- Closing an account
- Terminating an account
- Copy data objects into a cloud
- Copy data objects out of cloud
- Erase data objects on a cloud
- **VM (Virtual Machine):** Control-allocate VM instance
- **VM Control:** Manage virtual machine instance state
- **Query Cloud:** Provider capabilities and capacities

Cloud Interoperability Use Cases:

- Copy data objects between cloud providers
- Dynamic operation dispatch to IaaS clouds
- Cloud burst from data center to cloud
- Migrate a queuing-based application
- Migrate VMs from one cloud provider to another

Cloud Security Use Cases:

- Identity management: User account provisioning
- User authentication in the cloud
- Data access-authorization policy management in the cloud
- User credential synchronization between the enterprise and the cloud
- eDiscovery
- Security monitoring
- Sharing of access to data in a cloud

Role of OMG: In the Open Cloud Manifesto, OMG gives a more abstract set of use cases. These are much more generic than those published by NIST.

In addition, they relate more to deployment than to usage. The Changing Cloud Vendors and Hybrid Cloud use cases are of interest from a standards perspective because they are the main drivers for standards in cloud computing environments. For example, the Changing Cloud Vendors use case guides organizations that do not want to be in a vendor lock-in situation.

The following use cases are supported by OMG:

1. **End User to Cloud:** Applications running in the public cloud and accessed by end users.

2. **Enterprise to Cloud to End User:** Applications running in the public cloud and accessed by employees and customers.

3. **Enterprise to Cloud:** Applications running in the public cloud integrated with internal IT capabilities.

4. **Enterprise to Cloud to Enterprise:** Applications running in the public cloud and interoperating with partner applications (supply chain).

5. **Private Cloud:** A cloud hosted by an organization inside that organization's firewall.

6. **Changing Cloud Vendors:** An organization using cloud services decides to switch cloud providers or work with additional providers.

7. **Hybrid Cloud:** Multiple clouds work together, coordinated by a cloud broker that federates data, applications, user identity, security, and other details.

Role of DMTF: DMTF has also produced a list of 14 use cases specifically related to cloud management as follows:

1. Establish relationship

2. Administer relationship

3. Establish service contract

4. Update service contract

5. Contract reporting

6. Contract billing

7. Terminate service contract

8. Provision resources

9. Deploy service template

10. Change resource capacity

11. Monitor service resources.

12. Create service offerings

13. Notification of service condition or event

Conclusions: From the uses cases above, four types of use cases relate to consumer–provider interactions that would benefit from the existence of standards. These interactions relate to interoperability and can be mapped to the following four basic cloud-interoperability use cases:

1. **User Authentication:** A user who has established an identity with a cloud provider can use the same identity with another cloud provider.

2. **Workload Migration:** A workload that executes in one cloud provider can be uploaded to another cloud provider.

3. **Data Migration:** Data that resides in one cloud provider can be moved to another cloud provider.

4. **Workload Management:** Custom tools developed for cloud workload management can be used to manage multiple cloud resources from different vendors.

2.9 STANDARDS IN CLOUD COMPUTING

There is a need to address two issues—workload-migration and data-migration use cases. Standards that fulfill these two criteria are highly encouraged. This is because such standards would mitigate vendor lock-in concerns and also needs for standardization of virtual-machine image file formats and APIs for cloud storage.

Standardization for the user-authentication use case has an advantage where the user identities based on OpenID or authentication protocols based on OAuth, for instance, could be used across multiple providers that support these standards.

Standardization to support the workload-management use case would leverage any existing efforts related to the construction of workload management clients and scripts that could be used across multiple providers.

As we know, the cloud provides three types of services, basically—IaaS, PaaS, and SaaS. Next, we will discuss how these three main services benefit from standardization.

IaaS and Standardization: IaaS is a service model that would benefit greatly from standardization because the main building blocks of IaaS are workloads represented as virtual machine images and storage units that vary from typed data to raw data. For workload migration, standard efforts such as OVF and VHD would allow users to extract an image from one provider and upload it to another provider. Given that most IaaS providers allow consumers to install and run any OS, a more manual and time-consuming form of migration would be to retrieve the image from the current provider, create a new image on a new provider, and reinstall the software. This manual migration would not require standards as long as there is a way to retrieve the application state, for example, application data, files, and running processes from the source image and move it to a new image.

For data migration, standards efforts such as CDMI and the Amazon S3 API, which multiple providers support, would enable users to extract data from one provider and upload it to a different provider. If a provider implements these standard interfaces using SOAP- or REST-based protocols, the cloud will offer the advantages of ease of development and tool availability. However, these standards are more useful for raw data that is not typed, for example, virtual machine images, files, and blobs, because the cloud resource in this case acts as a container and usually does not require data transformation. For typed data, data migration would occur similarly to any other data migration task—users must extract data from its original source, transform it to a format compatible with the target source, and upload it into the target source, which could be a complex process. In addition, the effort required for transformation will also depend on factors such as the similarities between the target's and source's data storage technologies. Consider that moving from one SQL-compatible database to another will be easier than moving from an object database to a relational database and vice versa, and also the similarity of the interface operations such as two SOAP-based interfaces can have completely different operations.

PaaS and Standardization: The PaaS service model benefits less from standardization than IaaS. Organizations implementing PaaS will get benefits out of the development platform. The platform provides many capabilities out of the box, such as managed application environments, user authentication, data storage, and reliable messaging, in the form of libraries that can be integrated into applications. This functionality is tied to a specific language and run-time environment. For example, the Google App Engine supports applications written in Java, Python, and Go. MS Azure supports applications written in .NET and more recently written applications in Java2, PHP, and others. The incentives for PaaS adoption are basically rapid development and deployment, and the potential for these applications to serve a greater number of clients. Buying into PaaS means buying into a platform in the same way that organizations traditionally have and is based on added value, skills, cost, and so on, where providers can make applications more interoperable by selecting platforms that support more standardized tools and languages such as JDBC, ODBC, and SQL. For example, the default data store in the Google App Engine is the High Replication Data Store that offers automatic replication of data across data centers. A user can access the data store with a standard API or a low-level API. It is important to understand that the trade-off is where the standard API makes an application more portable but offers less control and less provider-specific value-added features than the low-level API, resulting in the lowest common denominator for features.

SaaS and Standardization: As we know, SaaS is a different model because it is a licensing agreement with a third-party software instead of a different deployment model for existing resources that range from data storage to applications. SaaS benefits from standardization are more limited than for PaaS. For SaaS offerings such as the salesforce.com CRM, the user is the end user. On the other hand, in other SaaS offering like Google Maps the user can be a developer who also is integrating functionality from these services into other applications. Here, again, standard APIs are useful because they facilitate the development process.

The SaaS provider has its own processing logic. In addition, the only field where SaaS would benefit from standardization is data storage because that is the most important concern for SaaS consumers. For instance, consider an online storage service that was shut down and the SaaS provider lost access to 45% of its customer data. In such a scenario, the consumer would have to extract its data from the SaaS provider, write logic to perform data transformations, and then upload the data to a new SaaS provider. The standardized APIs could make this task easier.

NOTE *Expecting PaaS and SaaS providers to standardize feature sets is equivalent to asking ERP software vendors to standardize feature sets.*

The question is do clouds require new standards? We will explore the answer here.

Interoperability refers to the ability of a collection of communicating entities to share specific information and operate on it according to agreed upon operational semantics. As explained earlier, even though a community desires standards for cloud interoperability, the reality is that existing standards efforts are so far focusing on portability only, that is, the ability to migrate workloads and data from one provider to another. Cloud interoperability, as defined by Brownsword, is the ability of resources on one cloud provider to communicate with resources on another cloud provider.

For IaaS, there are two basic use cases that exercise this service model's potential for interoperability:

USE CASE-1 (UC1): Workload W1 on Cloud C1 can communicate with Workload W2 on Cloud C2.

USE CASE-2 (UC2): Workload W1 on Cloud C1 can access Data Store (DS) in Cloud C2.

To support UC_1, the following conditions must be true:

1. Workload W_2 is accessible over the network and has a known address, URI, or other unique identifier.

2. Workload W_1 is authorized to communicate with Workload W_2.

3. Workload W_2 exposes an interface that Workload W_1 can use.

This is a common interoperability scenario between two systems, which does not require standards built especially for the cloud. Standards such as SOAP and REST and other existing user-authentication standards could support this scenario if the cloud meets the conditions as given above.

Note that once workloads are running in a cloud instance, they behave like any other server.

To support UC_2, the following conditions must be true:

1. DS is accessible over the network and has a known address, URI, or other unique identifier.

2. Workload W_1 is authorized to access DS.

3. DS exposes an interface that Workload W_1 can use.

In addition, this use case does benefit from standards for cloud data access such as CDMI and the Amazon S_3 API.

Basic Use Case

The basic use case that exercises the PaaS service model's potential for interoperability is similar to UC_1 for IaaS:

Application A_1 deployed on cloud C_1 can communicate with Application A_2 on cloud C_2. In addition, similarly to supporting UC_1 to support this use case, the following must be true:

1. Application A_2 is accessible over the network and has a known address, URI, or other unique identifier.

2. Application A_1 is authorized to interact with Application A_2.

3. Application A_2 exposes an interface that Application A_1 can use.

Note that this is also a common interoperability scenario that does not require standards built specifically for the cloud. The basic use case that exercises the SaaS service model's potential for interoperability is the same as for PaaS, except that it refers to interoperability between SaaS products instead of between applications. Interoperability between PaaS-deployed applications and IaaS workloads/data stores and SaaS products could also be supported the same way, if the cloud meets the conditions as given above. The bottom line is that existing standards such as those that support service-oriented systems can support real cloud interoperability.

System interoperability exists too at different levels. Technical interoperability is about exchanging data. Semantic interoperability is about exchanging meaningful data. Organizational interoperability is about participating in multi-organizational business processes. In addition, standards such as SOAP and REST enable technical or syntactic interoperability but do not guarantee semantic or organizational interoperability. Systems or data deployed inside cloud providers will have to rely on documentation or formal/informal agreements to provide meaning to the interaction (just as in any use case that requires systems to interoperate).

2.10 SCALABILITY AND FAULT TOLERANCE IN CLOUDS

1. **Resource Management:** When you deploy your application and services to the cloud, resource management provides the necessary virtual machines, network bandwidth, and other infrastructure resources. It is important to understand that if machines go down for hardware updates or because of unexpected failures, the cloud locates new virtual machines for your application automatically. Because you will only pay for what you use, you can start with a smaller investment. Doing so avoids incurring the typical upfront costs required for an on-premises deployment. This can be especially useful for smaller companies. In an on-premises scenario, small organizations might not have the data center space, IT skills, or hardware skills necessary to deploy their applications successfully. For example, the automatic infrastructure services that Microsoft Azure provides offer a low barrier of entry for application deployment and management.

2. **Dynamic Scaling:** The process of scaling out and scaling back your application depending on resource requirements is known as *dynamic scaling*. It is also known as *elastic scaling*. With cloud services, you create roles that work together to implement your application logic. For example, one web role could host the ASP.NET front end of your application. One or more worker roles could perform the necessary background tasks. One or more virtual machines hosting each role are called *role instances*. Requests are load balanced across these instances. It is important to understand that in this scenario, as resource demands increase, you can provision new role instances to handle the load. In addition, when demand decreases, you can remove these instances so that you do not have to pay for unnecessary computing power. There are also options for automatically scaling up and down based on pre-defined rules and policies. This is very different from an on-premises deployment where you must over-provision hardware to anticipate peak demands if you want more control over automatic scaling than the platform provides. It is also possible to scale-out websites and virtual machines. If your application requires fluctuating or unpredictable demands for computing resources, clouds like MS Azure allow you to easily adjust your resource utilization to match the load.

3. **High Availability and Durability:** Cloud vendors like MS Azure, provide a platform for applications that can reliably store and access server data through its storage services. Cloud applications like MS Azure have an MS Azure SQL Database for the same purpose. It ensures high availability of compute resources. For websites, you can meet the requirements of the Service Level Agreement (SLA) with only a single instance. For cloud services and virtual machines, you can meet the SLA requirements by having at least two instances per role or machine type. For virtual machines, the instances must be interchangeable and load balanced. It is the cloud vendor like MS Azure that monitors the actual hardware that hosts these virtual machines and instances. In addition, vendors like MS Azure are able to respond quickly to hardware restarts or failures by deploying new instances or moving application code and processing to other working hardware. The cloud vendors like Azure ensure high availability and durability for data stored by one of its storage services. MS Azure storage services replicate all data to at least three different servers. By default, this storage also replicates to a secondary MS Azure region. Similarly, the MS Azure SQL Database replicates all data to guarantee availability and durability.

4. **Highly Available Services:** Say there is an online store that is deployed in MS Azure. This online store is a revenue generator, so it is important and critical to keep it running. To achieve this objective, the Azure data center performs service monitoring and automatic instance management. The online store must also stay responsive to customer demand. The elastic scaling ability of MS Azure accomplishes this. During peak shopping times, new instances can come online to handle the increased usage. In addition, the online store must not lose orders. It is important to understand that both MS Azure and the Azure SQL Database provide highly available and durable storage options to hold the order details and state throughout the order life cycle. For the highest level of availability, you can deploy the same application to multiple MS Azure regions. In addition, it is possible to design a service that remains available even if an entire MS Azure region experiences a temporary failure. Doing this requires proper synchronization architecture and procedures for routing users.

5. **Periodic Workloads:** Some applications such as demos or utility applications are ones you want to make available for only several days or weeks. They need not run continuously. MS Azure allows you to easily create, deploy, and share that application. Once this purpose is achieved,

you can remove the application, and you are charged only for the time it was deployed.

Case Study: Consider a big company that runs complex data analysis of sales numbers at the end of each month. Although processing intensive, the total time required to complete analysis is at most two days. In an on-premises scenario, the server required for this work would be underutilized for the majority of the month. In MS Azure, the business would pay only for the time the analysis application is running in the cloud. Assume that the application architecture is designed for parallel processing. The scale out features of MS Azure would allow the company to create large numbers of worker role instances or virtual machines. Working together these can complete more complex work in less time. In this case study, you should use code or scripting to automatically deploy the application at the appropriate time every month.

NOTE   *To avoid charges for compute time, remove the deployment because just suspending the application is insufficient .*

6. **Unpredictable Growth:** All businesses have a goal of rapid and sustainable growth. However, growth is not easy to achieve if traditional on-premises models are used. If you do not meet the expected growth even after spending huge dollars then it means you have spent money on maintaining underutilized hardware and infrastructure. However, if growth happens more quickly than expected, you might be unable to handle the load. This results in lost business and poor customer experience. For smaller companies, there might not even be enough initial capital to prepare for or keep up with rapid growth. For example, say there is a small sports news portal (specialized part of a website) that makes money from advertising. Here, the amount of revenue is directly proportional to the amount of traffic that the site generates. In this case, the initial capital for the venture is limited. In addition, the company does not have the money required to set up and run its own data center. However, by designing the website to run on MS Azure, the company can easily deploy its solution as an ASP.NET application. The application will use the MS Azure SQL Database for relational data and blob storage for pictures and videos. If the popularity of the website grows dramatically, the company can increase the number of web role instances for its front end. The company can also increase the size of the Azure SQL Database service. The blob storage has a built-in scalability feature within MS

Azure. In addition, if business decreases, the company can remove any unnecessary instances. In addition, because its revenue is proportional to the traffic on the site, MS Azure helps the company to start small, grow fast, and reduce risk. If you use MS Azure in your company, then you have full control in finding out how you can manage your computing costs. You can decide to implement automatic scaling through the use of the Autoscale feature or through the use the Autoscaling Application Block. This can add or remove instances based on custom rules (pre-determined amounts). For example, you might have 8 instances during business hours and 4 instances during non-business hours. You can also keep the number of instances constant and only increase them manually through the web portal as demand increases over time. MS Azure provides you with the flexibility to make the decisions that are right for your business.

7. **Workload Spikes:** This workload pattern also works on the principle of elastic scale, as explained earlier. Consider the example of the sports news portal once again. Now, even because its business is steadily growing, there is still a possibility of temporary spikes or bursts of activity. For example, assume that another popular news outlet refers to the site. This means that the number of visitors to the site could dramatically increase in a single day.

Example 2: Consider a service that processes daily reports at the end of the day. When the business day closes, each office sends in a report that the company headquarters processes. However, because the process is only active a few hours each day, it is also a candidate for elastic scaling and deployment. In addition, MS Azure is suitable for temporarily scaling out an application to handle load spikes and then scaling back after the event has passed.

8. **Infrastructure Offloading:** It has been observed that most cloud scenarios make use of the elastic scaling of MS Azure. In addition, even applications that show steady workload patterns will incur a significant cost savings using MS Azure cloud services. It is difficult and costlier to manage your own data center because it is more expensive in terms of energy, people, skills, hardware, software licensing, and facilities. In addition, it can be difficult to understand how costs are tied to individual applications. MS Azure, however, brings those costs to a minimum and with more transparency as well.

For example, MS Azure Virtual Machines (VM) and Virtual Network (VN) provide an easier method for migrating on-premises servers and networks to the cloud. However, transitioning on-premises applications to cloud services or websites also alleviates the pressure on the on-premises data center. MS Azure and not these data centers are actually responsible for providing the required computing and storage resources for those applications. MS Azure provides a pricing calculator for understanding specific costs. It also provides a Total Cost of Ownership (TCO) calculator for estimating the overall cost reduction that clouds incur by adopting MS Azure.

9. Resource management, dynamic scaling, high availability, and durability are some of the main advantages of running applications in the cloud.

10. To ensure the highest levels of availability, for managing unpredictable growth, and for handling workload spikes, MS Azure is preferred.

11. Quick service, safe and secure service, multiple user access, development environment, and unlimited storage are some of its benefits.

12. Other benefits include fewer operational issues, more reliability, more flexibility, and innovative and easier communication among teams and customers.

2.11 CLOUD SOLUTIONS

The backing up of data to a remote, cloud-based server is known as *cloud backup* or *cloud computer backup*. This data is accessible from multiple distributed and connected resources that comprise a cloud. Cloud backup solutions enable enterprises or individuals to store their data and computer files on the Internet using a storage service provider rather than storing the data locally on a physical disk like a hard disk. Backup providers enable consumers to remotely access the service using a secure client login application to back up files from the customer's computers or data center to the online storage server using an encrypted connection. To restore or update a cloud back up, consumers need to use the service provider's specific client application or web browser interface. In addition, files and data can be automatically saved to the cloud backup service on a regular basis or the information can be automatically backed up any time changes are made. This is also known as *cloud sync*.

For enterprises, enterprise-grade cloud backup solutions are available that typically add required features such as archiving and disaster recovery.

2.12 CLOUD ECOSYSTEM

A cloud ecosystem is defined as a complex system of interdependent components, which work together to enable cloud services. By the term *complex* we mean both the traditional elements of a cloud (like software and infrastructure) as well as integration of consultants, third parties, partners, and anything related to their environments. When we say a *cloud ecosystem,* we say that there are five major actors:

1. **Service Providers:** These are the companies that offer cloud services to their customers and businesses. These companies run very big cloud data centers (CDCs to be discussed later). These CDCs host massively virtualized, redundant software and hardware systems. These may provide direct services to their customers. They are expert too in data center management and scalability.

2. **Software Vendors:** Cloud software (providing cloud services) runs differently than traditional software. These vendors may perform the same task but their architectures are different. In addition, sometimes an overlap exists between software vendors and the service providers. Software vendors observe that it is economically feasible to package software and hardware together in the data centers. This also optimizes service delivery in the cloud.

3. **Enablers/Implementers:** These are the vendors that offer services to provide end-to-end solutions with software integration from different vendors. Many companies buy software licenses from vendors but are unable to deploy it due to lack of expertise. Thus, enablers/implementers can solve this problem by providing consulting services for those purchased software licenses.

4. **Businesses:** Any business that can benefit from the cloud will implement it. This is because every business needs to maintain up-to-date IT and wants to minimize the costs involved.

5. **Independent Software Vendors:** They are experts in vertical scaling, that is, adding resources such as storage, processors, and so on, to expand processing capability. They build vertical applications on an existing platform. The cloud provides a great platform for these independent software vendors.

2.13 DUTY CYCLE

As we know, cloud data centers have several servers. This increases the energy consumption. These servers are designed to be overloaded and overdesigned for better reliability. They must support redundancy, error-correcting RAM, parity disk drives, (n + 1) power supplies, for example. All this functionality needs energy to cool and power it, light the data center, provide security, and so on. This concept of purposely overdesigning a true server for a constant reliable operation is known as a *duty cycle*.

2.14 CLOUD BUSINESS PROCESS MANAGEMENT

Every organization wants its processes to be current, up to date, and effective to make the company better. Business Process Management (BPM) is done during a crisis. This endeavor produces a suitable analysis and identifies the bottlenecks in a process. This can be easily done with the cloud. BPM involves six phases as shown in Figure 2.7.

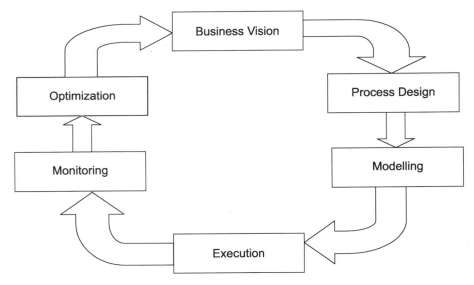

FIGURE 2.7 Cloud BPM.

The BPM phases can be described as follows.

Phase-1: Business Vision

The objectives and goals of any business are attached to its vision. Functions are planned around them. Each function is in turn associated with a list of processes. Thus, functions and processes help in achieving managerial goals. This is the job of the functional chief of the business.

Phase-2: Process Design

The existing processes and the required processes must be taken care of and designed. Proper process flow is needed.

Phase-3: Modeling

This phase takes design as an input and creates a business model.

Phase-4: Execution

The requirement is to develop software that executes all these steps properly. Buying is also an option but not an efficient solution. The process becomes more complex when we mix software and humans.

Phase-5: Monitoring

At this stage, it is necessary to track the identified processes, understand them, and build statistics on them. All customer transactions must be monitored and made better, if needed.

Phase-6: Process Optimization

Optimization here means minimization of potential bottlenecks, of costs, and so on, because this adds a "value" to the system.

Examples/Tools/BPM Software Products

IBM's Business Process Manager on the cloud offers business users a quick start. There is no need to maintain infrastructure. It delivers the BPMS (Business Process Management Service) as a PaaS service platform.

Other examples of BPM on the cloud are Oracle Fusion, Barium Live, Elite BPM Cloud, Billfish BPM, Cordys, and Appian BPM Suite. Commercial BPMSs available on the market today include IBM Business Process Management, Oracle BPM, and MS BizTalk. Open source software like Shark, Active BPEL, and jBPM are also available.

2.15 TESTING UNDER CONTROL

Cloud testing can be done through two different methods as follows:

1. Testing the Cloud

2. Testing on the Cloud

Testing the cloud involves both verification and validation of applications, environments, and infrastructure that are made available on a pay-per-use model. It refers to testing of private, public, and hybrid clouds, that is, whether these meet the customer's needs or not. Before migrating to the cloud, the applications in execution should ensure that the security and reliability of the applications are still in place.

On the other hand, testing on the cloud refers to the cloud infrastructure for performing traditional testing such as performance, load, stress, security, and compatibility. Testing on the cloud means testing applications that use resources such as the hardware, software, and infrastructure of the cloud. Testing-as-a-Service (TaaS) is a business model based on testing services on the cloud. It is an extension of testing on the cloud that delivers application-testing services in this pay-per-use model. TaaS is a new service model. It provides a provider provision to perform software testing of a given Application Under Test (AUT) in a cloud infrastructure based on customer demand.

As we know, testing is limited by budget, time, costs, exponential number of test cases, no reuse of tests, and so on. However, due to the unlimited storage of the cloud, rapid availability of infrastructure, increased scalability, and increased support for distributed testing environments, cloud testing is a better option. The cloud-based infrastructure should be able to form a test bed that is allocated to the testing community. Even cloud testing is bound by service-level agreements. A huge number of test cases and testing scenarios can be formed with the cloud. This is also called *on-demand testing*. Cloud computing represents TaaS as a service for SaaS and clouds. The intention is to validate SaaS in a cloud environment with software scalability, performance, security, and service-level agreements for a better quality in cloud-based applications. This kind of testing examines inter-operation capability and cloud compatibility between cloud services and applications in the cloud.

Advantages of TaaS

1. Reduced cost for cloud quality.

2. Minimum test cycle time.

3. Real-time online validations are possible because the cloud provides on-demand test services.

4. Easier to create a test environment.

5. Website testers can automate and speed up web testing processes.

6. Present day web applications are very complex. Testing these web applications is quite a challenging task. In general, cloud-based testing operates in a SaaS model. Thus, there is no need of investment in any hardware or software.

7. It further reduces test errors because the infrastructure that is provided is standardized.

8. Better scalability during testing as needed.

9. Both functional and non-functional testing of mobile applications can be done easily now because the cloud is geographically distributed.

Tools for Cloud Testing

Some of the popular tools for cloud testing are CloudTest, BlazeMeter, LoadStorm, Janova, Silk Performer CloudBurst from Borland, and HP Quality Center.

2.16 SECURITY ISSUES ASSOCIATED WITH CLOUDS

Some of the security issues associated with clouds are as follows:

1. In cloud computing, data is shared via the Internet. Data is stored in a data center so that users can access it from the cloud via these data centers. Thus, security is vulnerable. Hackers can easily hack the data by any means. Data should be protected during uploads into the data center.

2. Proper authentication of users is also required.

3. Timely availability of resources is also required.

4. Cloud-based applications are more vulnerable to attacks. A vulnerability is a weakness in the system that can be exploited by a threat. The systems need to be scanned properly.

5. Access control should be monitored so that only authentic users can use the cloud services.

6. Internet and mobile devices have provided new opportunities for data leaks.

7. A recent report by the IDC, which surveyed 244 respondents, found that security was the main challenge among cloud users today.

8. Another article in *InfoWorld* stated that "........megabytes of valuable customer or financial data could be compromised in just a few seconds if a rogue data-centric mash-up is created" [4].

2.17 CLOUD SECURITY CONTROLS

Several types of controls exist behind the cloud security architecture. They are as follows:

1. **Deterrent Controls:** These controls are set in place to prevent any purposeful attack on a cloud system. They are just like a warning sign and do not reduce the actual vulnerability of a system.

2. **Preventive Controls:** These controls manage vulnerabilities. If attacks were to occur, the preventive controls are in place to cover the attack and reduce the damage and violation to the system's security.

3. **Corrective Controls:** They are used to reduce the effect of an attack. These controls take action as an attack is occurring.

4. **Detective Controls:** They are used to detect any attacks that may be occurring to the system. In an event of an attack, the detective control will signal the preventive or corrective controls to address the issue.

SUMMARY

In this chapter, we studied cloud computing as Internet-based computing that allows users to access resources in a pay-per-use model. The cloud is a new paradigm of computing that is changing the ways that computational services are being used. A cloud computing platform has a Cloud Service Provider (CSP) with a large number of systems connected to it providing services to clients via the Internet. In addition to basic services, the cloud also provides TaaS, SeaaS, DaaS, MaaS as different services.

CONCEPTUAL SHORT QUESTIONS WITH ANSWERS

Q1. Define precloud computing?

Ans. 1 It is email access via a single computer, which also stores all email messages; for example, Microsoft Outlook or Outlook Express.

Q2. What is Zvent?

Ans. 2 Zvent is a web search engine for local events. You can upload a user event schedule into the Zvents database and then anyone in the user's area can find out what is scheduled on the calendar.

Q3. How are web-based projects managed?

Ans. 3 Different project management applications include additional functions useful in the management of group projects. These features may include group to-do lists, web-based file sharing, message boards, and time and cost tracking.

Q4. Name some task management applications in the cloud.

Ans. 4 HiTask, Zoho Planner, Basecamp, and GoPlan are some of the task management applications in the cloud.

Q5. Name some enterprise-level web-based expense reporting applications.

Ans. 5 Concur, ExpensePoint, and TimeConsultant are some of them.

Q6. Name some web-based presentation programs.

Ans. 6 Google Presentations, Preezo, and Zoho Show are some of them.

Q7. Name some web-based project management applications.

Ans. 7 AceProject, Basecamp, and onProject are some of them.

Q8. What is Google Calendar? How is it different from Yahoo Calendar? In addition, explain what the Apple MobileMe Calendar is?

Ans. 8 Google Calender is a free, fully featured, and easy to use calendar application that lets the user create both personal and shared calendars which makes it useful for tracking business groups, family, and community schedules. However, in Yahoo Calendar there is an additional Add Task button.

The MobileMe calendar is a web-based calendar that can be accessed from any computer connected to the Internet, through a Mac or Windows.

Q9. Name some web-based database applications.

Ans. 9 Dabble DB, MyWebDB, QuickBase, TeamDesk, and Zoho Creator are some of them.

Q10. Name some web-based word processing applications.

Ans. 10 Google Docs, ajaxWrite, Adobe Buzzword, KBdocs, and Zoho Writer are some of them.

Q11. What are the different types of cloud application requirements?

Ans. 11 There are two types of cloud-based requirements:

(a) Functional requirements

(b) Non-functional requirements

Functional requirements should cover the following points:

(a) Required features

(b) Business goals

(c) User requirements

Non-functional requirements should cover the following points:

(a) Security

(b) Response time

(c) Services available

(d) Backups to other clouds

(e) Extension to hybrid clouds

(f) Localization

(g) Compatibility with other cloud platforms

(h) Support for end-user devices like mobile devices

Q12. What is SOA for cloud applications?

Ans. 12 It is defined as a set of methodologies to design a cloud application in the form of interoperable units or services. These services are business functionalities that are built as software modules or pieces of code. These services can be reused for different other purposes within the cloud. Other cloud developers are free to use and combine these services to create new applications. These functionalities or services are loosely coupled units (non-associated). SOA (Service-Oriented Architecture) can be used to support communication between services too like data transfers. Each of these interactions between services is self-dependent. SOA enables large applications to be broken into smaller components. They can be developed independently. Each of these smaller components is known just as a service. Later these components are assembled or loosely coupled to meet business needs. Thus, we can define a SOA application as a modular, loosely coupled set of services designed to meet business needs. Because the services (or components) can be easily ported to another platform, they have high cross-platform interoperability. SOA services are ideal for deployment in the cloud.

Q13. What are the benefits of SOAs used for project work?

Ans. 13 According to the Gartner report,(a) More than 60% of SOA projects had a positive impact on their organizations (to grow revenue). (b) SOA projects give positive returns within 10 months.(c) SOA reduces the cost of building IT systems.(d) SOA improves a developer's productivity too.

Q14. KR V & V company developed an application that they had to deploy as an SaaS and make it available to the global user community. Later the project manager found that there was a need to do performance testing with a large number of users because the user load was very high. However, the KR V & V company could not afford to procure costly performance automation tools for the purpose. What should this company do?

Ans. 14 KR V & V company should approach another company offering TaaS services. This new TaaS-based company decides to conduct performance testing using HP's Quality Center on a cloud computing platform by paying only resource usage charges. The testing is done and then the application is deployed as a SaaS.

Q15. Name some cloud-based testing service vendors.

Ans. 15 Cloud service vendors such as SOASTA, HP Cloud, Testhouse, Compuware, Load Impact, and Neotys are some of the companies that allow simulation of large web applications and checks their behavior on a cloud platform.

Q16. Write down the steps that are followed in using cloud-testing services.

Ans. 16. The following tests are followed when using cloud-testing services: S1: Select cloud test service provider S2: Develop user scenarios to test S3: Design test cases S4: Leverage cloud servers S5: Conduct testing S6: Analyze tests

Q17. What is Media Cloud?

Ans. 17. Media Cloud is a system that lets you see the flow of the media. Media Cloud automatically builds an archive of news stories and blogs from the web, applies language processing, and gives you ways to analyze and visualize data. This field is still in its infancy and more research needs to be done.

Q18. Summarize the following:

(a) CloudStack

(b) Computing on demand

(c) Cloud sourcing

(d) Cloud analytics

(e) Resiliency

(f) Provisioning

(g) Cloud governance

Ans. 18.

(a) CloudStack: It is an open source monolithic software platform that groups computing resources to build public, private and hybrid Infrastructure as a Service (IaaS) clouds. It handles network, storage, and nodes that form a cloud infrastructure. The CloudStack platform is used to install, manage, and configure cloud computing environments. Some of the benefits of CloudStack are as follows:

(a) Pay-per-use metering

(b) Network management

(c) AJAX-based web GUI for management

(d) Built-in high availability for hosts

(e) Virtual routers, firewalls, and load balancers

(b) Computing on Demand (CoD): This is an enterprise model that maintains computer resources that are made available to the user enterprises as needed. Since demand for resources is dynamic, the vendor must maintain sufficient resources and this is a challenge for them. Vendors such as HP, MS, IBM, Salesforce, Amazon, and Sun Microsystems all provide on-demand services because it allows them to create elastic environments for better scaling.

(c) Cloud Sourcing: A method in which cloud services and products are outsourced to one or more cloud providers. It is the future of cloud computing. This concept allows organizations to procure their entire IT infrastructure from the cloud.

(d) Cloud Analytics: This is also called *SaaS-based Business Intelligence* (BI). It is a type of cloud service model wherein the elements of data analytics are provided with the help of a private or public cloud only. Such applications are provided on a utility-based or pay-per-use model. For example, there are hosted data warehouses, cloud-based social media analytics, and SaaS BI. Cloud analytics will combine some or all of the service models of the cloud to deliver solutions.

(e) Resiliency: This is defined as the ability of a data center and its components to continue operating in case of any damage such as a power outage, malfunctioning of equipment, or natural disasters like earthquakes, for example.

(f) Provisioning: This is the process of allocating a cloud provider's resources to the customer. Through the term *provisioning*, we mean what, how, and when an organization can provide cloud services. It helps in managing workloads, resources, tasks, and processes. It can be done in three ways:

1. **Dynamic provisioning** (cloud bursting)

2. **Contractual Provisioning** (the customer and contractor sign an agreement for required services)

3. **Self-provisioning/cloud self-service** (the customer fills out a form, pays through a credit card, and then he gets resources within a few hours)

(g) Cloud Governance: This is defined as a sharing of responsibility between the cloud provider and the user of cloud services. The main objective of cloud service governance is to protect data and applications that are located far away (remotely). It manages contracts for SLAs and charging through credit cards. However, to make use of fine-grained services, governance will help. It also involves defining policies, design policies, and implementation policies.

Q19. How are clouds accessed?

Ans. 19. There are three methods to access the cloud:

(a) Platforms

(b) Web applications

(c) Web APIs

(d) Web browsers

Platforms: Show how a cloud computing environment is delivered to the end user. The objective is to support dynamic website development, web services, and web applications. Newer technologies such as AJAX (Asynchronous JavaScript and XML) creates interactive web applications [1,2]. Similarly, Python Django is a free open source web application framework developed in the Python language. It is used to create complex websites with database connectivity.

Web applications: Google Apps and Google Apps Premier Edition.

Web APIs: API stands for Application Programming Interface where there is a set of programs to access a web-based program. For example, GoGrid has an API that allows developers to perform monitored communications with their cloud hosting infrastructure. It supports languages such as JAVA 2, Python, PHP, and Ruby.

Similarly, the Apex API is very popular enterprise web service used today.

Web Browsers: Popular web browsers like Chrome, IE 8, Firefox, and Safari, for example, are all used to getting cloud services through the Internet.

Q20. Distinguish between a traditional data center and a cloud data center.

Ans. 20 The following table distinguishes the two data centers:

Traditional Data Center	Cloud Data Center
1. It has thousands of different applications.	1. It has a fewer number of applications.
2. It has mixed a hardware environment.	2. It has homogeneous hardware environment.
3. It supports multiple management tools.	3. It supports standardized management tools.
4. It needs frequent application patching and updating.	4. It has minimal application patching and updating.
5. It includes complex workloads.	5. It includes simple workloads.

CHAPTER REVIEW QUESTIONS

Q1. Explain different cloud standards. In addition, describe security standards.

Q2. What is a cloud ecosystem? Explain.

Q3. What is cloud outsourcing?

Q4. What is cloud testing? On what factor does cloud testing depend?

Q5. What are cloud testing challenges?

Q6. Summarize cloud testing tools.

Q7. Explain TaaS.

Q8. Name some web-based spreadsheet applications.

[Hints: NumSum, Sheetster, Zoho Sheet, EditGrid, etc.]

Q9. Distinguish between functional requirements and non-functional requirements?

3

VIRTUALIZATION TECHNOLOGY IN THE CLOUD

3.1 INTRODUCTION

Virtualization can be defined as the abstraction of four computing resources—storage, processing power, memory, and network (I/O). Conceptually, it is similar to emulation where a system pretends to be another system, whereas virtualization is a system pretending to be two or more of the same system type. Today virtualization is better than parallelism. It has helped to evolve the cloud data center techniques and tools. These technologies manage the dynamic data center infrastructure as well. Virtualization partitions the physical resources of the underlying physical server into multiple virtual machines with different workloads. The virtualization layer schedules and allocates the physical resources and makes each virtual machine think that it completely owns all of the physical resources of the underlying hardware. This technology is very useful for cloud computing because it improves resource utilization by multiplexing many virtual machines on one physical host. Thus, these machines can be scaled up or down on-demand, and thus, better management techniques are required.

The complex applications of today cannot be feasibly run on the existing physical hardware alone. It is, however, possible to implement, test, and run large applications with the help of this virtualization technology. Virtual technology creates virtual versions of hardware, operating systems (OSs), networking devices, and storage devices. Therefore, many guests OSs can now be run on a single physical machine called a *host machine* and multiple guest applications run on a single server called a *host server*. Additionally, this technology allows a single physical resource to work as multiple virtual resources and multiple physical resources as a single virtual resource. Virtualization may be achieved through several methods including hypervisors, virtual storage engines, and virtual networks, for example. With respect to virtualization technology, a cloud may be defined as a virtualization of resources that can be maintained and managed by itself. This maximizes the rate of utilization for each server and decreases the number of servers. Technologies like Xen and VMware, VPNs, and so on, are some of the virtualization technologies today. Thus, virtualization decouples (software is put under a separate container so that it is isolated from the OS) the software from the hardware.

3.2 EVOLUTION

1. IBM introduced virtualization technology in the 1960s wherein users could run more than one operating system on a mainframe.

2. Next, IT companies added servers in their data centers.

3. However, servers were very inefficient at that time because 100% CPU utilization could not be achieved.

4. To achieve better resource utilization, resource scheduling began to be implemented.

5. VMware, an IT vendor, changed the dynamics of computer optimization and a new stage was set for modern virtualization.

3.3 VIRTUALIZED ENVIRONMENT CHARACTERISTICS

The following are the three characteristics of virtualization:

1. **Partitioning:** Many applications and OSs are supported on a single physical system by partitioning/separating the available resources.

2. **Isolation:** If one virtual instance crashes, it will not affect other virtual machines. Data is not shared between one virtual container and another.

3. **Encapsulation:** A virtual machine (VM) can be represented as a single file. An encapsulated process could be a business service. This encapsulated VM can be presented to an application as a complete entity. Therefore, the encapsulation can protect each application so that it does not interfere with another application.

3.4 CREATING A VIRTUALIZED ARCHITECTURE

During virtualization, software known as a *Virtual Machine Monitor* (VMM) or a *Hypervisor* is used.

What is a Hypervisor?

A hypervisor is an operating system (OS) that knows how to act as a traffic policeman to guide processes in an orderly manner. It is set at the lowest levels of the hardware environment. In cloud computing, it is necessary to support several types of OSs and a hypervisor is the correct method to do this. It helps you to show and use the same application on several systems without having to physically copy that application onto each system. With virtualization technology, it is possible to use the hypervisor to split the physical computer's resources. The resources can be split 50–50 or 80–20 between two guest operating systems. The advantage here is that the hypervisor does all the heavy lifting. The guest OS does not care that it is running in a virtual partition. It thinks it has the computer all to itself. There are three different types of hypervisors:

1. **Native Hypervisors:** They sit on the hardware platform directly. They give better performance to the end users.

2. **Embedded Hypervisors:** They are integrated into a CPU on a separate chip.

3. **Hosted Hypervisors:** They run as a different software layer above both the hardware and the OS. This type is useful for both private and public clouds because it improves performance.

Two different virtualization structures are thus formed as follows:

1. **Hosted Virtualization.**

2. **Bare-Metal Virtualization.**

Let's study each of these structures with their pros and cons.

1. Hosted Virtualization Structure

This structure enables users to run different guest application windows on top of a base OS (e.g., the Windows x86 OS) with the help of a VMM or hypervisor. Examples include the VMware Workstation and Mac Parallels Desktop (shown in Figure 3.1).

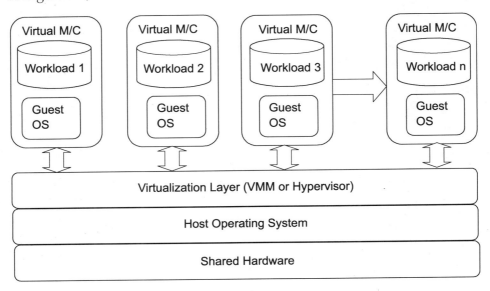

FIGURE 3.1 Layered hosted virtualization structure.

It is clear from Figure 3.1, that the virtualization layer partitions the physical resources of the underlying physical server into multiple virtual machines with different workloads. This virtualization layer schedules and allocates the physical resources and makes each virtual machine think that it owns all of the underlying hardware physical resources including the processor, disks, RAMs, and so on.

This type of structure enables you to run different guest applications in Windows on your own on top of a base OS with the help of the hypervisor or VMM. The I/O requests must pass through the host OS.

Operation: The virtual or guest operating systems (see Figure 3.1) has limited access to the I/O devices. Only a defined subset of I/O devices with guest systems may be used. The I/O connections to a given physical system are owned only by the host systems while their emulated view is presented by the VMM to every single guest machine running on the same base system. The VMM, however, will not provide any view of generic devices to the virtual machines. Only generic devices such as a Network Interface Card (NIC) and CD-ROM drives can be emulated. Non-generic devices do not update the VMM about themselves. In these structures, another facility called *pass-through* is also provided that allows individual virtual machines to access USB devices directly from the port. This structure takes into account a number of software components to make I/O access possible.

For example, the VMware Workstation uses a low-level VMM, then a driver, and after that, the VMApp (a user-application component) to direct the I/O requests from the guest machines. Finally, the I/O requests are passed through the host system by the VMApp.

Advantages of a hosted structure

1. Here, multiple guest systems are easily installed, configured, and executed.

2. Next, a hypervisor or VMM is installed. You can run several guest systems on different platforms without any need for extra physical resources.

3. It is also possible to run these different VMMs so that they are shared across different PCs. They require no customization because the drivers provided by the host OSs establish communication with the low-level hardware.

Disadvantages of a hosted structure

1. This structure is not capable of providing pass-through to many I/O devices.

2. The performance of hosted systems may be downgraded as the I/O request made by the guest systems must be passed through a host OS.

3. This structure does not support real-time operating systems because there is full control of the host OS in the scheduling of its applications and the hypervisor.

2. Bare-Metal Virtualization Structure

With this structure, the hypervisor/VMM is installed to establish direct communication with the hardware that is being used by the base system. Here, the hypervisor or VMM does not rely on the host system for pass-through permissions (see Figure 3.2).

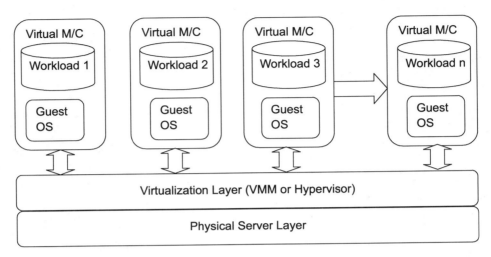

FIGURE 3.2 Layered bare-metal virtualization structure.

Operation: With this structure, different options exist to access I/O devices from the guest systems. The VMM can have direct communication with the I/O devices because the host OS is not relied upon. A shared usage of I/O devices between these virtual systems needs the hypervisor to have a low-level driver (to communicate with the device). It is necessary for the VMM to have the ability to emulate the shared devices for the guest virtual machines. The hypervisor uses a partitioning technique to access the I/O devices. Partitioning is defined as the process of assigning individual I/O devices to particular VMs, which improves the performance of the I/O system. VM intervention is also kept to a minimum because the guest systems access the partitioned I/O devices directly through their native drivers.

Advantages of a bare-metal structure

1. It is possible to run a real-time OS on systems with a bare-metal virtualization structure. This is possible because of the partitioning of only the I/O devices.

2. A single hardware platform can be made to run real-time and general purpose OSs in parallel. Thus, the bare-metal-type VMMs can be used for binding the interrupt latency and allowing deterministic performance.

Disadvantages of a bare-metal structure

1. The VMM must include supporting drivers for hardware platforms along with the drivers for sharing the I/O devices among the guest systems.

2. It is difficult to install the VMM in this structure model compared to hosted structures because the VMMs are not installed on top of a base OS.

3.5 CLOUD DATA CENTER

Data centers with 10,000 or more servers on site are considered a Cloud Data Center (CDC). The main features of CDCs are as follows:

1. They are constructed for a different purpose.

2. They are created at different times.

3. They are built to a different scale.

4. They are not constrained by the same limitations as in traditional data centers.

5. They perform different workloads from those of traditional data centers.

6. CDCs support many customers with a large number of servers executing a single application.

7. They optimize IT productivity and resource utilization.

8. They allow superior scale-up and scale-out server/storage consolidation and virtualization.

9. They have lower costs and higher utilization.

10. They achieve reduced operations costs through streamlining management and provisioning pooled resources.

Table 3.1 distinguishes between traditional and cloud data centers:

TABLE 3.1 Traditional CDCs versus Cloud Data Centers

Traditional Data Center	Cloud Data Center
1. It has thousands of different applications.	1. It has a fewer number of applications.
2. It has a mixed hardware environment.	2. It has a homogeneous hardware environment.
3. It supports multiple management tools.	3. It supports standardized management tools.
4. It needs frequent application patching and updating.	4. It has minimal application patching and updating.
5. It includes complex workloads.	5. It includes simple workloads.

The cost of creation for CDCs depends on three factors [Albert Greenberg et al]:

1. **Labor Costs:** Constitute 6% of the total costs of a CDC.

2. **Power Distribution and Cooling:** About 20% of the total cost.

3. **Computing Costs:** About 48% of the total cost.

Data centers consume large amounts of electricity. According to data provided by HP:

- 100 server racks can consume 1.3MW of power.

- Another 1.3MW are needed by the cooling system.

- Total cost is $2.6 million per year.

Furthermore, CDCs affect the environment in terms of CO_2 emissions from the cooling systems. Dynamic resource management can improve resource utilization and also reduce energy consumption in data centers.

Koomey also observed that computer energy efficiency appears to be doubling every 18 months (just as Moore's law states that computing power increases every 18 months). High energy costs and high carbon footprints are involved because huge amounts of electricity are consumed to power and cool servers hosted in these data centers. The carbon impact on the environment must be minimized. This must be done by cloud service providers. For example, the data created and uploaded on the Facebook website is more than 100 million units per day, in the form of photos, and so on. These are stored only in data centers (on servers). To run these data centers, air conditioning is required to prevent overheating. This again increases energy consumption. There exists a symbiotic association between energy consumption and resource utilization. They are strongly coupled.

In 2006, the EPA (Environmental Protection Agency) reported that data centers consumed 1.5% of the total U.S. electricity consumption (double of that of 2000).

With the increase in data center growth, the Department of Energy believes that data centers may be consuming up to 3% of total European electricity by 2020.

A data center consists of three parts:

- Servers
- Data storage
- Local Area Network (LAN)

The data center is connected to the network through switches, routers, and gateways, which all work on electricity. It is expected that by 2020, an exponential amount of data may be stored in these data centers. This raises the issues of managing data, testing the data, and mining it. The energy consumed by these networking devices, the location of data centers, and so on, are some of the reasons for high-energy consumption.

As per the U.S. report, the adoption of cloud computing could save $12.3 billion a year by 2020 and potential carbon reductions of 85.7 million metric tons per year by 2020. With VM technology, the VM can be moved between physical nodes allowing dynamic migration of VMs. When VMs do not use all the resources provided, they can be logically resized and idle nodes can be switched off. According to current CPU utilization, dynamic reallocation of VMs provides higher energy savings compared to static allocation policies. Thus, lower energy consumption is now possible.

Better research must be done on generating electricity using eco-friendly methods so that cloud carbon footprints can be reduced. Facebook encountered great opposition from Greenpeace because it was using nuclear energy and coal to power its massive data centers. Instead, green energy should be used for these data centers. There is a need to adopt green architecture and to make the cloud greener.

Cloud data centers are huge. Many have hundreds of square feet of space. MS Azure's data center takes up as much space as ten football fields. Clouds are expensive. The expense for a single CDC can be in the hundreds of millions of dollars. Many cloud regions are actually comprised of two or more distinct data centers. CDCs are showing up in clusters around major Internet hubs. Cloud providers have under-invested in emerging markets with high Internet use. Some data center regions have servers grouped inside containers each containing 1800–2500 servers. The locations of some data centers are:

1. North America (California, Chicago, Virginia etc.)

2. South America (Brazil)

3. Asia (China, Hong Kong, Singapore)

4. Europe (Dublin, Ireland, Amsterdam, Netherlands)

5. Japan (Osaka, Saitama)

6. Oceania (Sydney, Wales, Victoria, Melbourne)

These CDN nodes are located in 24 countries.

3.6 RESILIENCE

Resilience is defined as the ability of a data center and its components to continue operating in case of any damage such as a power outage, malfunctioning of equipment, or natural disasters like earthquakes, and so on. It creates an environment that protects valuable applications, services, and the information infrastructure. It ensures regulatory compliance by providing a resilient network infrastructure that supports security, improved Service-Level Agreements (SLAs), and application delivery-optimization services.

3.7 AGILITY

Agility facilitates the adoption of new IT strategies like SOA (Service Oriented Architecture), virtualization, and on-demand computing, which allow faster responses to changes.

3.8 CISCO DATA CENTER NETWORK ARCHITECTURE

This architecture includes the following:

1. **Networked Infrastructure:** 10 Gigabit Ethernet, Fibre Channel Switching on intelligent server farms, server fabric, storage networking platforms, DWDM, SONET, and SDH optical transport platforms.

2. **Interactive Devices:** Storage fabric services, compute services, security services, application delivery, and integration services.

3. **Management Framework:** Configuration, security, provisioning, change, and fault management services.

Cisco created the Cisco WebEx Collaboration platform. It became the core system after integrating with a SaaS platform. Cisco uses this platform to add unified communications as a service.

3.9 STORAGE

Hundreds of cloud storage systems exist. NetApp provides a unified storage architecture that allows customers the flexibility to manage, support, and scale their environment using one set of knowledge bases and tools. NetApp customers use these products from remote offices for the data center, collecting, distributing, and managing data from all locations and applications at the same time.

NetApp benefits include the following:

1. Stores the maximum amount of data at minimal cost.

2. Fifty percent lower capacity requirements without sacrificing performance or resiliency.

3. Achieves 100% utilization.

4. Fifty percent or greater reduction in power, cooling, and space requirements.

5. Manages twice as much data without using personnel.

6. Maximizes the value of existing storage systems.

7. One solution for all environments and highly flexible.

8. One skill set to manage.

9. Everything works together (synergy).

10. Everything can do more.

11. Simpler administration because one process works everywhere.

12. Easier to deploy.

3.10 THIN PROVISIONING AND CLOUD PROVISIONING

These are the processes of allocating a cloud provider's resources to the customer. By the term *provisioning*, we mean what, how, and when an organization can provide cloud services. Provisioning helps in managing workloads, resources, tasks, and processes. It can be done through three methods:

1. **Dynamic provisioning:** (Cloud bursting).

2. **Contractual Provisioning:** (A customer and contractor sign an agreement for required services).

3. **Self-provisioning/Cloud self-service:** (A customer fills out a form, pays through a credit card, and then he gets the resources within a few hours).

Provisioning is the process of providing users with access to data and technology resources. It refers to enterprise-level resource management. During provisioning:

1. Users are given access to data repositories or granted authorization to systems, applications, and databases based on a unique user identity.

2. Access rights and privileges are monitored and tracked to ensure the security of the company's resources.

3. Users are provided with accounts, proper access to those accounts, and all other resources needed to manage those accounts. With reference to a client, provisioning can be thought of as a form of customer service.

What are thin provisioning and cloud provisioning?

Thin provisioning: This functionality allows the consolidation and automated process of allocating just "the exact required amount" of server space at the time it is needed. It is mostly used in centralized large storage systems such as SANs and also in storage virtualization environments where administrators plan for both current and future storage requirements and also over-purchase capacity, which can result in wasted storage. Thin provisioning is designed to allocate exactly what is needed, exactly when it is needed so it removes the element of "paid for but wasted" storage capacity. If more storage is needed, then additional volumes can be attached to the existing consolidated storage systems.

Cloud provisioning: This functionality entails developing the processes for interfacing with the cloud's applications and services as well as auditing and monitoring those who will have access and utilize the resources. It is to be decided upon before deployment in the cloud where some services will reside in a public cloud and some will be behind a private cloud. The most common reference to cloud provisioning is when a company seeks to transition some or all of its existing applications to the cloud without having to significantly re-architect or re-engineer the applications.

3.11 ASSET MANAGEMENT

With an increasing number of regulations imposed on the financial services space, its participants are expected to have a material impact on the technology and operational decisions they will need to make. These reforms will have a substantial influence on more than 4000 brokerage firms and an estimated 8500 investment managers globally. The new regulations are likely to push some firms to further migrate functions that are traditionally maintained within the walls of the asset management firms. Chief financial officers will continue to apply pressure to heads of IT and operations to seek ways to trim costs in response to continued market uncertainty and reduced profitability.

In December 2010, Gartner's Data Center Conference was held and it was reported that:

- Fifty-five attendees responded to a poll asking, "By 2015, how would you describe your virtualization progress?" The responses showed a majority of users in the financial services space leaning toward greater use of private and hybrid clouds.

If asset managers are compelled to divert scarce and valuable resources to overcoming operational issues and deficiencies in their investment management IT platforms, then their prospects for increased productivity will weaken. According to the Tower Group, asset management functions that are likely to benefit from cloud computing are real-time, regulatory and performance reporting, data management and valuation as well as compliance management and audits.

3.12 MAP REDUCE CONCEPTS—A LOGICAL VIEW

MapReduce (MR) is a framework for processing parallelizable programs across huge data sets using large numbers of computers (nodes), collectively referred to as a *cluster* (if all nodes are on the same LAN and use similar hardware) or a *grid* (if nodes are shared across geographically and administratively distributed systems and use more heterogeneous hardware). Computational processing can occur on data stored either in a file system (unstructured) or in a database (structured). MapReduce can take advantage of the locality of data, processing data on or near the storage assets to decrease transmission of data. MapReduce is a programming model for processing large data sets with a parallel, distributed algorithm on a cluster. The MapReduce system/infrastructure/framework is orchestrated by marshaling the distributed servers, running different tasks in parallel, and managing all communications and data transfers between the various parts of the system. MapReduce libraries have been written in many programming languages, for example, Apache Hadoop.

Google uses it for processing large amounts of raw web data. MapReduce uses two functions:

1. **Map Function:** This function processes a key-value pair, which is associated with the input data and generates a set of intermediate key-value pairs.

2. **Reduce Function:** This function merges all intermediate values that are related with the same intermediate key.

MapReduce is simple data processing using large clusters. MapReduce processes many terabytes of data on several thousands of machines. It is highly scalable. Task scheduling, input partitioning, message passing, and so on, can all be done now by MapReduce (unlike parallel programming).

MapReduce Functionality

MapReduce works by following three phases as follows:

1. **Map Phase:** This phase uses an input reader that outputs data one record at a time. It makes use of the map() function. When the map phase runs, it calls the reader to obtain one input record at a time and then implements the map() function to each record. The map() function outputs key-value pairs to the shuffle stage.

2. **Shuffle Phase:** This phase groups all pairs having the same key together and outputs a single list of values for every particular key.

3. **Reduce Phase:** This phase uses the reduce() function. When this phase runs, the reduce() function will be called for each unique key existing in the shuffled intermediate data set. This function takes a key and the sequence of values related with that key and outputs a new value depending on the input. The result is sent to the output writer.

It is not necessary that the number of Reduce tasks be equal to the number of Map tasks. For example, say a database of 1.1 billion people exists. The objective is to calculate the average number of social contacts a person has, based on age. Then in SQL one may write as follows:

SELECT age AS Y, AVG (contacts) AS A

FROM social.person GROUP BY age ORDER BY age;

On the other hand, using MapReduce, the K1 values could be integers 1 through 1100, each representing a batch of 1 million records, the K2 key value could be a person's age in years, and this computation can be achieved. The MapReduce system, would line up 11,000 Map processors and would provide each with its corresponding 1 million input records. The Map step would produce 1.1 billion <Y, N> records, with Y values ranging between, say 8 and 103. The MapReduce system would then line up 96 Reduce processors by performing shuffling operation of the key/value pairs due to the fact that we need an average per age and provide each with its millions of corresponding input records. The Reduce step would result in the much reduced set of only 96 output records <Y,A> which would be put in the final result file, sorted by Y. Thus, Map() and Reduce() look like the following:

function Map is

    input: integer K1 between 1 and 1100, representing a batch of 1 million social.person records

for each social.person record in the K1 batch **do**

    let Y be the person's age

    let NN be the number of contacts the person has

    produce one output record <Y,N>

  repeat

end function

Similarly, we can write the Reduce() functions as follows:

  input: age (in years) Y

  for each input record <Y,N> **do**

  accumulate in S the sum N

  accumulate in C the count of records so far

  repeat

  let A be S/C

  produce one output record <Y,A>

end function

MapReduce (MR) is a prominent example of PaaS. It allows users to:

- Define their own specific map and reduce algorithms.

- Utilize the respective PaaS infrastructure with its MR supporting usage modes like elasticity, communication, and so on.

Due to the big umbrella constituting different types of cloud infrastructures, it is mandatory to implement the MR framework for each of them. For example, the SAGA (Simple API for Grid Applications) MapReduce provides MR development and a runtime environment that is implemented in SAGA. The SAGA standard and SAGA implementations provide higher-level programming abstractions to developers. At the same time, it shields them from the heterogeneity and dynamics of the underlying infrastructure.

The main advantage of a SAGA-based approach is that it is infrastructure independent. It provides control over deployment, distribution, and runtime decomposition.

3.13 CLOUD GOVERNANCE

Governance is the process of controlling access to a service with the help of policies, tracking services using storage, and logging and monitoring the execution of those services. Thus, cloud governance means implementing the principles and policies of cloud services. The objective is to protect data and applications that are located far away (remote distance).

Need for Cloud Governance

1. Risks are reduced.

2. It provides a structure for organizing several projects and avoiding any redundant work.

3. It helps in managing consumer/provider relationships.

4. It helps in managing contracts for SLAs and charge-backs.

5. The SOA governance will define the essential governance and management process for the consumer or provider environments, including project management, policy management, and service management. The number of services and problems with their implementation will make service governance more compelling.

6. There is lack of cloud governance process models for the complete cloud life cycle including cloud strategy, planning, modeling, architecture, on boarding and off boarding, cloud portability, cloud requirements analysis, and operations and sustainment.

3.14 HIGH AVAILABILITY AND DISASTER RECOVERY

High Availability and Disaster Recovery Cloud Services (HA & DR Cloud) provide a way for clients to get a high availability or disaster-recovery computer capacity without having to own their own system for this functionality. It can be used as an off-site solution for clients who own local systems.

HA Cloud: The HA Cloud is a mirroring service where all of the data is mirrored to a system located in the Iptor Data Center. The mirrored system contains exactly the same data as the production system.

DR Cloud: This is a service where Iptor is providing an empty partition that only runs the system software. In case of disaster, the capacity of the partition can be increased and the clients system can be installed in the partition.

The HA and DR Clouds are hosted at Iptor's secure data center in Sweden. High availability answers queries such as the following: Do you want low or no downtime during planned maintenance of your production system? Do you want to reduce the number of disasters? Disaster Recovery answers queries such as the following: Do you want a fail safe for unexpected incidents? Do you want an easy and flexible solution for securing important data during natural disasters?

3.15 SERVER VIRTUALIZATION

Server virtualization is defined as the process of partitioning a physical server into smaller virtual servers to help maximize your server resources. In this method, the resources of the server itself are hidden or masked from the users, and software is used to divide the physical server into multiple virtual environments called *virtual* or *private servers*. This is in contrast to a dedicated single server. The advantage here is that instead of requiring a separate computer for each web server, dozens of virtual servers can co-reside on the same computer. Thus, one physical machine is partitioned into many virtual servers. Each small server is called a *virtual private server*. Virtual servers are cheaper compared to dedicated servers. Here, the physical server is called a *host* while the virtual servers are called *guests*. The core of this virtualization technique is a hypervisor/VMM or virtual machine monitor. It is a thin layer and it intercepts the OS calls to the hardware. It abstracts physical resources from the systems that run on top of it. It is also possible to move a virtual server from one physical machine existing in a network to any other physical machine located in a different network. This process is known as *migration* (see Figure 3.3).

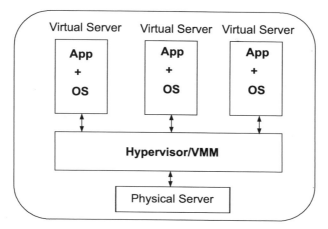

FIGURE 3.3 Server virtualization method.

Hypervisors or VMMs also have two types:

1. **Native (or bare-metal):** These types of VMMs are directly installed onto the hardware (just like we install a normal OS) on a single server. The benefits here are high performance and lower overhead. These run on hardware with the guest OSs that runs on them. Examples include VMware ESXi, Citrix XenServer, and MS Hyper-V.

2. **Non-Native:** These types of VMMs run on the current OS with the guest OS running at the third level above the hardware. These are installed directly onto an existing OS. The benefits here are lower performance and higher overhead. Examples include MS Virtual PC, VMware Workstation, and Oracle Virtual Box.

In fact, server virtualization can be carried out with three different methods:

1. Paravirtualization

2. OS virtualization/container-based virtualization

3. Hardware emulation

Let's study each of these methods.

I. Paravirtualization: This is a technique in which the hypervisor or VMM communicates with the guest OS to improve the performance and efficiency of virtual systems. The non-virtualized instructions are replaced by modification in the OS kernel through the technique of paravirtualization. Hypercalls are used for communication with the VMM or hypervisor virtualization layer. The hypercalls to the virtualization layer replace the non-virtualizable OS instructions. This paravirtualization technique is different from full virtualization. In full virtualization, the OS is not aware of being virtualized, while in paravirtualization, the OS is aware that virtualization being applied to it. In paravirtualization, several OSs run on a single set of hardware by making use of the system resources effectively. Paravirtualization efficiencies result in better scaling. Thus, virtualization means running modified versions of the OSs.

Applications

Paravirtualization has several applications in capacity management, disaster recovery, partitioning, and migrations.

Advantages of Paravirtualization

1. Each virtual server can be independently rebooted.

2. It reduces costs because less hardware is required.

3. It also conserves space through consolidation because several machines can be consolidated into one server running multiple virtual environments.

4. It uses resources to its fullest and thus saves on cost.

Disadvantages of Paravirtualization

1. It is necessary to have access to the OS source code. This is because this method requires revision of the guest OS so that it interacts easily with the paravirtualization interfaces, like the modified Linux kernel used by the Xen project. Here, the processor and memory are utilized in the Xen architecture through the Linux kernel whereas virtualization of the I/O devices uses guest OS device drivers that are customized.

2. Support and maintainability are also issues here because it is necessary to have permissions for deep modifications in the OS kernel.

3. There is no support for a non-modified OS kernel.

   II. Operating System Virtualization/Container-based: This is defined as a process of customizing a standard OS to run different applications that are controlled by different users on a single system at a time. Here, operating systems do not interfere even if they exist on the same system. The OS is modified in such a way that it works as several different individual systems. It is used to relocate critical applications to any other running OS instance. For example, Oracle Solaris and SWsoft's Virtuozzo use OS virtualization.

III. Hardware Emulation: If it is necessary to run an unsupported OS within a VM then the administrator can use this technique. The emulation layer will manage the traffic between the physical machine and the VM hardware. The VM will not have direct access to the server hardware. This method is less efficient than paravirtualization and in general, it is used to debug and verify a System-Under-Design (SUD).

Disadvantages of Hardware Emulation

1. It is necessary to install device drivers between the VMM and the hypervisor because the VMM acts as an interpreter between the physical machine and the hypervisor.

2. It is difficult for a normal user to install these devices.

3. If VMM drivers do not exist for any of the devices, then it will not work in such a virtualized environment.

In general, server virtualization has several advantages; for example, it is easier for software developers to work as they need not install the OS on their PCs. In addition, VMs allow sandboxing, better space utilization in the cloud data center, no collisions between applications, and corrections or changes can be made at the infrastructure level.

On the other hand, server virtualization has certain disadvantages; for example, it degrades performances, security is reduced because there are more vulnerable points introduced, an experienced administrator is needed, and virtualization is not a part of the software.

3.16 VM MIGRATION SERVICES

Please refer to Section 3.15 of this chapter.

3.17 NETWORK VIRTUALIZATION

Some of the definitions of network virtualization are as follows:

"The process of combining software network resources and hardware network resources into a single unit is known as Network Virtualization."

"It is the process of managing and monitoring the entire computer network as a single administrative unit from a single software dependent on the administrator."

"The process of running of multiple networks on the same network device where each network runs in isolation as if it is working individually and using the entire network resources is called network virtualization."

The main objective is to allow users and systems to have secure and efficient sharing of network resources. Thus, all network services are treated as a single pool of resources that can be accessed regardless of the physical components. This provides better network efficiency and productivity. For example, MS Azure uses this method. Azure enables you to create a logically isolated section and securely connect it to your on-premises data center or a single client machine using an IPSec connection. Network virtualization makes it easy for you to take the advantage of Azure's scalable, on-demand infrastructure while providing connectivity to data and applications. This means that there will be n-virtual machines using cloud services and that they will communicate with MS Azure via the virtual network.

Advantages

1. Parameters like QoS (Quality of Service), bandwidth throttling, for example are easily managed by the administrators.

2. Easier to maintain security because systems are logically separated.

3. Network components like switches, hubs, firewalls, and load balancers can be shared now rather than buying them repeatedly. This reduces costs too.

Applications

This technique is useful in cloud computing, Storage Area Networks (SANs), and core-based processors.

3.18 APPLICATION VIRTUALIZATION

In this type of virtualization, we create a virtual machine that works separately at the application level and operates in a manner similar to a normal machine with a set of applications. You can run your applications on these virtual machines as if you are running your applications on a physical machine. This was the origin of the Java Virtual Machine (JVM), which brought about this concept. The application is provided to the user from a remote (far away) location, that is, a central server. There is no need to install that particular application on the user's local system. Thus, the application installation and the client system are isolated from each other as shown in Figure 3.4.

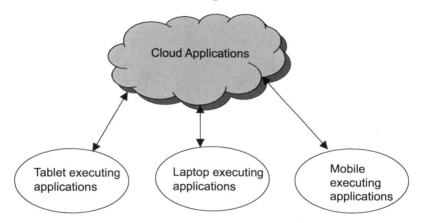

FIGURE 3.4 Application virtualization at work.

Application virtualization has two types:

(a) Remote application virtualization

(b) Downloaded/streamed application virtualization

In remote virtualization, remote applications (applications that are far away) are used to run on a server. The end users can use these applications through a network protocol. This network connection must always work properly for the remote application to work.

On the other hand, virtualized applications get executed on the user's local system with the help of streaming, that is, whenever an application is requested by the end user, it gets downloaded to the local system. After downloading is over, the streamed application will also work without any Internet connection.

Advantages

1. Lower resource requirements.

2. It protects the OS and other codes from errors.

3. It is possible for a system to run different versions of the same application simultaneously without any problems.

4. OS migrations (studied earlier) are made easier.

5. Lower threat to the security of the system.

6. It improves delivery and compatibility of applications by encapsulating them away from the underlying OS on which they are executed.

Disadvantages

1. Applications like Windows do not execute in a VM because they were not developed for this.

2. Applications that interact with auxiliary devices may not function properly.

3. Multimedia hardware still does not operate in virtual environments.

Applications

Applications include VMware, ThinApp, and MS APP-V.

3.19 LOCAL DESKTOP VIRTUALIZATION

Local desktop virtualization implementations run the desktop environment on the client device using hardware virtualization or emulation. Any type of hypervisor may be used. These implementations provide an end user with the desktop environment to provide access to authorized applications irrespective of the application location. The OSs, user data, and the applications are now hosted on servers in the organization's data center and the users are allowed to access their desktops from anywhere and at anytime. It can be done in two ways:

(a) Server-hosted desktop virtualization

(b) Client-hosted desktop virtualization

In server-hosted desktop virtualization, the operating environment will be hosted on a server that is located in a data center and accessed by the end user over the LAN or WAN. On the other hand, in client-hosted desktop virtualization, the operating environment works locally on the user's system hardware. The hypervisor software will be installed on the client system that will allow one desktop to run multiple OSs. For example, this implementation can be used to run Windows 7 on top of OS X on an Intel-based Apple Mac, using a hypervisor like VirtualBox, Parallels Desktop for Mac, or VMware Fusion. This works because both operating systems use the same x86 architecture and because it is possible to run Windows on a PowerPC-based Mac using a virtual PC.

Advantages

1. It is useful for environments where continuous network connectivity cannot be assumed.

2. It is also useful where application resource requirements can be better met by using local system resources.

3. There is more security because the administration is centralized.

4. The user can access the desktop environment through the LAN, WAN, and so on.

5. The capacity of the servers is higher.

Disadvantages

1. They do not always allow applications developed for one system architecture to run on another.

2. Clients must have a network connection to access their virtual desktops.

3. The numbers of OSs (their count) that can be supported by desktop virtualization products are limited.

4. Handling of graphics, audio, and videos is not easy.

3.20 VIRTUALIZATION ADVANTAGES AND DISADVANTAGES

As we know, virtualization is the kind of service for which a company only wants to spend during the tenure of using the service. The Internet is the best example of this.

Advantages

1. **Maximum Resource Utilization:** Because the cloud works on a pay-as-per-use model, organizations can use the maximum amount of the required resources. Even resource management and infrastructure maintenance is reduced.

2. **Minimizing Hardware Costs:** You need not install large servers, bigger disk spaces, or costlier databases because these services can be accessed anytime and anywhere virtually. This reduces hardware costs.

3. **Using Multiple Systems:** Because the VMM or hypervisor provides a platform for more than one OS to work, the use of multiple systems is easier with the help of virtualization.

4. **OS Services:** If you are running an OS from your laptop but you need some type of service from another OS, then you can avail yourself of the service through virtualization.

5. **Better Testing:** Because virtualization allows you to install more than one OS, you can test new software releases without requiring separate, dedicated systems for testing. Even if this OS fails for some reason, you can still test software with other systems running on the same machine.

6. **Better security:** Different virtualized computers do not have separate security concerns. Virtualization will increase the security of your systems.

7. It reduces the data center operating costs.

8. It reduces the physical infrastructure costs.

9. It provides easy migration and balancing of workloads.

10. Utilization of resources increases by 20% to 80%.

11. There is reduction in power consumption.

12. Easier disaster recovery because the cloud is virtualized.

13. Faster provisioning and deployment, and better resiliency and easier movement of VMs from one server to another server.

14. No need for the user to stay with only one vendor server service.

Disadvantages

1. Internet connection is a must.

2. Flexibility is at stake.

3. Less security.

4. Higher cost of running a virtualization program.

5. Costlier software licensing when virtualization is also needed.

6. More powerful machines are required.

7. If the hardware fails, all the virtual machines will be affected.

8. Customer support is also lacking.

3.21 BLOCK- AND FILE-LEVEL STORAGE VIRTUALIZATION

Storage virtualization helps in achieving location independence by abstracting the physical location of the data. The virtualization system presents the user with a logical space for data storage and handles the process of mapping it to the actual physical location. The process of defining the physical storage from several network storage devices acting like a single storage device is known as *storage virtualization* or *cloud storage*. Just as data storage has increased in size and numbers, storage virtualization also comes in three flavors now: networked-based storage virtualization, host-based storage virtualization, and storage-device-based virtualization.

File virtualization is a field of storage virtualization operating at the computer file level. It involves uniting multiple storage devices into a single logical pool of files. A primary driver behind file virtualization is the desire to shield users and administrators from the complexity of the underlying storage environment. Other goals include simplified management, more efficient capacity usage, and allocation and reduced management costs.

Advantages

1. It is simple to design and code.

2. It supports any storage type.

3. It improves storage utilization.

4. No thin provisioning limitations.

5. Storage space can be reclaimed.

6. Less energy is needed.

Disadvantages

1. The software is unique to each OS.

2. Storage utilization is only optimized on a per host basis.

3. Replication and data migration are only possible to local hosts.

4. It does not allow the vendors to interoperate easily.

5. It is a complex network system.

6. If a single network fails, the entire network is lost.

3.22 MOVING VIRTUALIZATION TO CLOUDS

Virtualization of almost everything is being applied to every field of IT. It is becoming a requirement in managing a data center from a service-delivery point of view. Cloud computing is the next stage of development of virtualization. The types of workloads that surround a cloud data center are mixed; for example, web transactional systems, messaging systems like email and chat, business intelligent systems, document management systems, and workflow systems. Cloud computing can help with these systems. Thus, virtualized environments must be developed, analyzed, implemented, tested, and protected like traditional systems.

3.23 CLOUD SECURITY FUNDAMENTALS

Some of the requirements or issues for cloud data security are as follows:

1. Researchers have pinpointed that storing data in and fetching data from resources (devices, machines) behind the cloud is a novel form of database outsourcing. Due to rapid developments in the field of network technology, the cost of transmitting a terabyte of data over long distances has decreased. In addition, the total cost of data management is five to ten times higher than the initial acquisition costs. Thus, the need for outsourcing of database management systems to third parties has been felt. This minimizes economies of scale as well.

2. Cloud storage services are concerned about losing data or data corruption. Thus, better data security should be provided to reassure the user.

3. If data is stored far away (remotely), then a web browser is the most widely used approach to access the data. Therefore, web security plays a vital role today.

4. Due to recent developments in the fields of high speed networking and larger bandwidth connections, more and more multimedia data is being stored and shared in cyber space. The security requirements for applications in these fields are different from other applications.

5. Security is a major concern in cloud computing. A public cloud offers services to many customers (tenants), so complete security and logical isolation should be provided to each tenant at each layer (network, computation, and storage).

6. All traffic between the customer edge router to the cloud gateway (an entry point to a cloud facility) must be completely secure and ensured as such.

7. IT professionals are perplexed about how to take advantage of cloud computing.

8. Security is broadly classified under two categories:

    (a) Protecting the assets, that is, the hardware, software, and network infrastructure of IT systems.

    (b) Protecting data.

9. Security-as-a-Service (SaaS) delivers monitoring services, patch updates, virus control, and so on, over the Internet.

10. According to Gartner, "Security delivered as a cloud-based service will be more than triple in many segments by 2013."

11. Traditional software-based security and SaaS are compared in Table 3.2:

TABLE 3.2 Comparison of Traditional Security and Cloud Security

Traditional Software-based Security	SaaS Provider
It is necessary to buy, install, and implement servers and applications.	No costs are involved for IT hardware and software because the resources are shared in the cloud.
It is difficult to detect threats on hosts.	Efficient threat detection with cloud-based servers.
Each host needs to be updated.	24/7 real-time updates available.
Lower latency (delay) is involved.	More latency (delay) exists because traffic is re-routed through a security provider.
Larger teams are required.	Fewer IT staff are required.

12. Data being transmitted can be encrypted for more security. Protocols like HTTP, HTTPS, FTP, and so on, may be used.

13. Data that is at rest like data on disk also needs to be secured. The process of securing data either in the cloud or outside the cloud is similar. The data at rest in a cloud need not be encrypted because it may avoid searching of that specific data. However, data in transit must be encrypted for better security.

14. Even after deleting data from a hard disk, some quantity of data remains on a storage device. This data is called *residual data*. This data is left either due to normal deletions or due to the physical properties of the storage medium. This may result in a loss of sensitive data. In cloud computing too, this loss may be experienced even if the company uses a cloud service. When we delete data from a hard disk, it is not actually deleted from the disk; rather the operating system removes that particular entry from its directory or database. This means that the data that is deleted will still remain on the hard disk until that location is

again used by the OS for storing new data. Sometimes this overwritten data may not be removed completely.

15. There are three methods for removing residual data:

   (a) **Clearing:** This is the process of overwriting at the location of the deleted data with some strings.

   (b) **Purging:** This does not provide opportunities for accessing the residual data.

   (c) **Destruction:** This involves the physical destruction of the hard disk.

3.24 CLOUD SECURITY SERVICES

Authentication, Authorization, Auditing, and Accountability (AAAA) are the four As that affect cloud software assurance and they are as follows:

1. **Authentication:** This is defined as the testing or reconciliation of evidence of a user's identity. It establishes the user's identity and ensures that users are who they claim to be. For example, a user presents an identity (User ID) to a login screen and then has to provide a password. The system authenticates the user by verifying that the password corresponds to the individual presenting the ID.

2. **Authorization:** This refers to the rights and privileges granted to an individual or process that enables access to resources and information. After the user's identity and authentication are established, authorization levels determine the extent of the system rights that a user has.

3. **Auditing:** To maintain operational assurance, companies may use two methods: system audits and monitoring. These methods can be used by the cloud customer, the cloud provider or both, depending on the asset architecture and deployment. A system audit is a one-time or periodic event to evaluate security. However, monitoring refers to an ongoing activity that examines either the system or the users, for example, intrusion detection. IT auditors can be two types: internal and external auditors. Internal auditors work for a company while external ones do not. Their main job is to have system and transaction controls. An audit trail or log is a set of records that collectively provide documentary

evidence of processing. It is used in tracing from original transactions forward to related records and reports. These logs should record the transaction date and time, the person who processed the transactions, at which terminal, and some security events related to the transaction.

4. **Accountability:** This is defined as the ability to determine the actions and behaviors of a single individual within a cloud system and to identify that particular individual. Audit trails and logs support accountability. Accountability is related to the concept of non-repudiation where an individual cannot successfully deny the performance of an action.

3.25 DESIGN PRINCIPLES

Secure cloud design is predicated on certain golden rules. These are enumerated as follows:

Principle 1: (Principle of Least Privilege)

This principle states that, "an individual, process or other type of entity should be given the minimum privileges and resources for the minimum period of time required to complete a task."

This principle mitigates the opportunities for unauthorized access to sensitive information.

Principle 2: (Principle of Separation of Duties)

This principle states that, "the completion of a specified sensitive activity or access to sensitive objects is dependent on the satisfaction of a plurality of conditions."

For example, authorization would require signatures of more than one individual. Separation of duties forces collusion among entities in order to compromise the system.

Principle 3: (Principle of Defense in Depth)

This principle states that, "the application of multiple layers of protection wherein a subsequent layer will provide protection if a previous layer is breached."

The Information Assurance Technical Framework (IATFF), an organization sponsored by the National Security Agency (NSA), has produced a document entitled as *Information Assurance Technical Framework (IATF)*, which provides complete guidance on the concepts of defense in depth.

Principle 4: (Principle of Fail Safe)

This principle states that, "…if a cloud system fails, it should fail to a state in which the security of the system and its data are not compromised."

Say we make a system default to a state in which a user or process is denied access to the system. A complementary rule would be to ensure that when the system recovers, it should recover to a secure state and not permit unauthorized access to sensitive information.

Principle 5: (Principle of Economy of Mechanism)

This principle states, "promote simple and comprehensible design and implementation of protection mechanisms so that unintended access paths do not exist or can be readily identified and eliminated."

Principle 6: (Principle of Complete Mediation)

This principle states that, "every request by a subject to access an object in a computer system must undergo a valid and effective authorization procedure."

This mediation must not be suspended even when the information system is being initialized, being shutdown, being restarted, or is being maintained. Mediation includes identification of the identity making an asset request, verification of the request, applying of proper authorization procedures, and testing of these requests for being authentic or not.

Principle 7: (Principle of Open Design)

This principle states, "let the cloud design be an open access cloud design system that can be evaluated by experts to provide more secure authentication."

Principle 8: (Principle of Least Common Mechanism)

This principle states that, "a minimum number of protection mechanisms should be common to multiple users, as shared access paths can be sources of unauthorized information exchange."

Shared paths that provide unintentional data transfers are known as *covert channels*. Thus, this principle promotes the least possible sharing of common security mechanisms.

Principle 9: (Principle of Psychological Acceptability)

This principle refers to "the ease of use and intuitiveness of the user interface that controls and interacts with the cloud access control mechanisms."

Users must be able to understand the GUI and use it without having to interpret complex instructions.

Principle 10: (Principle of Weakest Link)

This principle states that, "the security of the cloud system is only as good as its weakest component."

Thus, it is important to identify the weakest mechanisms in the security chain and to improve them so that risks to the system are reduced to an acceptable level.

Principle 11: (Principle of Leveraging Existing Components)

This principle states, "ensure that the security mechanisms are operating at their optimum design points as this will improve security."

To increase cloud security using this principle means to partition the system into defended sub-units and then if the security mechanism is penetrated for one sub-unit, it will not affect the other sub-units and damage to the resources will also be minimal.

3.26 SECURE CLOUD SOFTWARE REQUIREMENTS

The requirements for secure cloud software are related to non-functional issues like minimizing vulnerabilities and ensuring that the software will perform as required even under attack. This goal is different from security functionality in software, which addresses areas that are derived from the information security policy like identification, authentication, and authorization. As we know, requirements engineering is the process of determining customer software expectations and needs, and it is conducted before the software design phase. The requirements must be correct, unambiguous, quantifiable, and detailed. Goertzel et al. at DACS, in the United States says that all software shares the following three security needs:

1. It must be dependable under anticipated operating conditions and remain dependable under hostile operating conditions.

2. It must be trustworthy in its own behavior and in its inability to be compromised by an attacker through exploitation of vulnerabilities.

3. It must be resilient enough to recover quickly to full operational capability with a minimum of damage to itself, the resources, and the data it handles and the external components with which it interacts.

3.27 POLICY IMPLEMENTATION

The term *policy* can mean different things, for example, security policies on a firewall that refer to the access control and routing list information. Another example is that of standard procedures and guidelines that are also put under a *global information security policy.*

Policy implementation is not just an exercise on a paper. It may also be life-saver during disaster or it might be a government requirement. A policy can also provide protection from liability due to an employee's action or it can control access to trade secrets. Policies are considered the first and highest level of documentation from which the lower level elements of standards, procedures, and guidelines flow. This does not mean that higher-level policies are more important than the lower elements. These higher-level policies, which reflect the more general policies and statements, should be created first in the process, for strategic reasons and then more tactical elements can follow. Management should ensure the high visibility of a formal security policy because almost all employees at all levels will in some way be affected, major organizational resources will be addressed, and many new terms, procedures, and activities will be introduced.

The first policy of any policy creation process is the senior management statement of policy. It is a general, high-level policy that acknowledges the importance of the computing resources to the business model; states support for information security throughout the enterprise, and commits to authorizing and managing the definition of the lower-level standards, procedures, and guidelines.

Regulatory Policies: These are security policies that an organization must implement due to compliance, regulation, or other legal requirements. These companies might be financial institutions, public utilities, and so on.

Advisory Policies: These are security policies that are not mandated but strongly suggested with serious consequences defined for failure to follow them. A company with such policies wants most employees to consider these policies mandatory.

Informative Policies: These are the policies that exist simply to inform the reader. There are no implied or specified requirements and the audience for this information could be certain internal or external parties although this does not mean that the policies are authorized for public consumption but that they are general enough to be distributed to external parties (like vendors accessing an extranet) without a loss of confidentiality.

3.28 CLOUD COMPUTING SECURITY CHALLENGES

When an organization migrates to consuming cloud services like public services, then much of the computing system infrastructure will now be under the control of a third-party Cloud Service Provider (CSP). These challenges must be addressed only through management activities. Security managers must be able to determine what detective and preventive controls exist to clearly define the security of the organization.

Some general management processes will be required that include the following:

1. Security policy implementation

2. Computer intrusion detection and response

3. Virtualization security management

4. Virtual threats

5. VM monitoring from the host

6. VMM from another VM

7. VM backdoors

These processes are explained as follows.

Security Policies: These are the foundation of a sound security implementation. Often organizations will implement technical security solutions without first creating this foundation of policies, standards, guidelines, and procedures.

Computer Intrusion Detection and Response: These include the appropriate parties to take action in order to determine the extent of an incident's severity and to remediate the incident's effects. According to NIST, an organization should address computer security incidents by developing an incident-handling capability.

Virtualization Security Management: Threats to the virtualized infrastructure are evolving very rapidly. The virtual machine (VM), Virtual Memory Manager (VMM), and hypervisor or host OS are the minimum set of components needed in a virtual environment.

Virtual Threats: In virtualized systems, some of the threats are very general in nature because they are inherent threats to all computerized systems like Denial-of-Service/DoS attacks. Many VM vulnerabilities stem from the fact that vulnerability in one VM system can be exploited to attack other VM systems or the host systems because multiple virtual machines share the same physical hardware. Many companies are now conducting security analysis and proof-of-concept attacks against virtualized systems. Some of the vulnerabilities in VM systems include:

- **Shared Clipboard Technology:** Allows data to be transferred between VMs and the host. It provides a means of moving data between malicious programs in VMs of different security realms.

- **Keystroke Logging:** Some VM technologies enable the logging of keystrokes and screen updates to be passed across virtual terminals in the virtual machine, writing to host files, and allowing the monitoring of encrypted terminal connections inside a VM.

- **VM Monitoring from the Host:** Because all network packets coming from or going to a VM pass through the host, the host may be able to affect the VM by starting or stopping, pausing and restarting VMs; monitoring resources available to the VMs like CPU, memory, disk, and so on; adjusting the number of CPUs, amount of memory, number of virtual disks and number of virtual network interfaces available to the VM; and viewing, modifying, and copying data stored on VM virtual disks.

- **Virtual Machine Monitoring from Another VM:** Usually, VMs should not be able to directly access one another's virtual disks on the host. However, if a VM platform uses a virtual hub or switch to connect the VMs to the host, then intruders may be able to use a hacker technique known as *ARP Poisoning* to redirect packets going to or from the other VM for sniffing.

- **Virtual Machine Backdoors:** A backdoor covers communications channel between the guest and host that could allow intruders to perform potentially dangerous operations.

3.29 CLOUD SECURITY MECHANISMS

Virtualized resources, geographically dispersed servers, and co-location of processing and storage pose challenges and opportunities for cloud providers and users. The Open Security Alliance (OSA) defines security architecture as "the design artifacts that describe how the security controls are positioned and how they are related to the overall IT architecture."

Several factors affect the implementation and the performance of cloud security architecture. These can include regulatory requirements, adherence to standards, security-management information classification, and security awareness.

3.29.1 Encryption, PKI, SSO, IAM

Even cloud data needs to be encrypted so that communications are more secure. Calls to remote servers should be examined for embedded malware and digital certificates should be employed and managed. A certification process can be used to bind individuals to their public keys as used in public key cryptography. A certificate authority (CA) acts as a notary by verifying a person's identity and issuing a certificate that vouches for a public key of the named individual. This certification agent signs the certificate with its own private key. Thus, the individual is verified as the sender if that person's public key opens the data. To verify the CA's signature, its public key must be cross-certified with another CA. The standard X.509 standard defines the format for public key certificates. This certificate is then sent to a repository, which holds the certificates and Certificate Revocation Lists (CRLs) that denote the revoked certificates.

Figure 3.5 shows how digital certificates are used in a transaction between a subscribing entity and a transacting party.

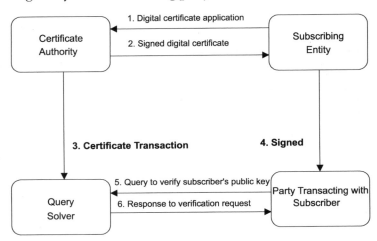

FIGURE 3.5 A transaction with digital certificates.

The integration of digital signatures and certificates and other services required for e-commerce is called the *Public Key Infrastructure (PKI)*. These services provide integrity, access control, confidentiality, authentication, and non-repudiation for e-transactions. The PKI includes the following elements:

- Digital certificates

- Certificate authority (CA)

- Registration authorities

- Policies and procedures

- Certificate revocation

- Non-repudiation support

- Time stamping

- Lightweight Directory Access Protocol (LDAP)

- Security-enabled applications

The digital certificate and management of the certificate are the major components of PKI. The purpose of a digital certificate is to verify to all that an individual's public key—posted on a public key ring—is actually his or hers. A trusted third-party CA can verify that the public key is that of the named individual and then issue a certificate attesting to that fact. The CA accomplishes the certification by digitally signing the individual's public key and associated information.

Certificates and CRLs can be held in repository with the jobs defined between them. The users can then access the repository for this information. In a PKI, a repository is also called a *directory*. The directory contains entries associated with an object class. An object class can refer to individuals or other computer-related entities. The class defines the attributes of an object. Attributes for PKIs are defined in RFC 2587. The X.509 certificate standard defines the authentication bases for the X.500 directory. The X.500 directory stores information about individuals and objects in a distributed database residing on network servers.

SSO or Single Sign-On addresses the complex situation of logging on multiple times to access different resources. Users must remember several passwords and IDs; they might take shortcuts in creating them that could leave them open to exploitation. In SSO, a user provides one ID and password per work session and is automatically logged on to all of the required applications. For SSO security, the passwords should not be stored or transmitted in clear. SSO applications can run either on a user's workstation or on authentication servers.

Advantages of SSO

Some advantages include the ability to use stronger passwords, easier administration of changing and deleting the passwords, and less time required to access resources.

Disadvantages of SSO

Once users obtain access to the system through the initial login, they can freely roam the network resources without any restrictions.

Authentication mechanisms include items like smart cards and magnetic badges. Strict controls must be enforced to prevent a user from changing configurations that another authority sets. SSO can be implemented by using scripts that replay the user's multiple logins or by using authentication servers to verify a user's identity and encrypted authentication tickets to permit access to system services.

3.30 VMWARE ESX MEMORY MANAGEMENT

This is a VMM (Virtual Machine Monitor) platform that is the basis of many utility or cloud computing environments. VMware is pioneer in the virtualization market. Its ecosystem of tools ranges from server and desktop virtualization to high-level management tools. ESX is a VMM from VMware. It is a bare-metal hypervisor. This means that it installs directly on the physical server whereas others may require a host OS. It provides advanced virtualization techniques for CPU, memory, and I/O. Through memory ballooning and page sharing, it can over-commit memory thereby increasing the density of VMs inside a single physical server.

NOTE *Several other VMM platforms also exist including Xen, KVM, UM-Linux, and VirtualBox.*

SUMMARY

We studied virtualization whereby one or more physical servers can be configured and partitioned into multiple independent virtual servers, all functioning independently, and appearing to the user to be a single physical device. Such virtual servers do not physically exist and can thus be moved around and scaled up or down on the fly without affecting the end user. Computing resources have become granular which provides the end user and operator with benefits including on-demand self-service, broad access across multiple devices, resource pooling, rapid elasticity, and service metering capabilities. Any user who has permission to access the server can use the server's processing power to run an application, store data, or perform any other computing task. Instead of using a PC every time to run the application, the individual can run the application from anywhere in the world, because the server provides the processing power to the application and the server is also connected to a network via the Internet or other connection platforms to be accessed from anywhere.

CONCEPTUAL SHORT QUESTIONS WITH ANSWERS

Q1. What is cloud storage? Why do we use it? What are the risks associated with it? Name some common cloud storage services.

> **Ans. 1** The first form of web-based data storage is called *cloud storage*. It is a form of network data storage where data files are stored on multiple virtual servers. The best example of cloud storage is Amazon.com's Simple Storage Service (S3). There are three benefits of using it: scalability, reliability, and lower costs. However, there are some risks also associated with it like security risks, scalability risks, user error, and access problems. Some popular cloud services include Amazon S3, Egnyte, ElephantDrive, Mosso, myDataBus, and Windows Live SkyDrive.

Q2. What are cloud classification criteria?

> **Ans. 2** Different types of criteria may be used to classify an information object:
>
> 1. **Value:** These criteria are used for classifying data in the private sector. If the information is valuable to an organization then it needs to be classified.
>
> 2. **Age:** The classification of information might be lowered if the information's value decreases over time. Within the U.S. DoD, some classified documents are automatically declassified after a predetermined time period has passed.
>
> 3. **Useful Life:** If the information has been made obsolete (old) due to new information or substantial changes in the company, the information can often be declassified.

4. **Personal Association:** If information is personally associated with a specific individual or is addressed by a privacy law, it might need to be classified. For example, investigation information that reveals important names might need to remain classified.

Q3. What are the various pricing methods used by cloud service providers?

Ans. 3 Several methods of pricing are used by cloud providers including CPU capacity, RAM hours, storage space (GB of data), bandwidth, and subscription-based pricing. Newer billing models are also used including IDC cloud billing research and the GoGrid Cloud hosting plan.

Q4. Define a cloud ecosystem.

Ans. 4 A cloud ecosystem is a complex system of interdependent components, which work together to enable cloud services.

Q5. What is SOAP?

Ans. 5 SOAP provides a way for a program executing in one kind of OS to communicate with the program executing in the same or another OS with the help of WWW, HTTP, and XML as the methods of information exchange.

CHAPTER REVIEW QUESTIONS

Q1. Use the World Wide Web as an example to illustrate the concept of resource sharing, client, and server. Resources in the WWW and other services are called URLs. What do the initials URL denote? Give examples of three different types of web resources that can be called by URLs.

Q2. A service is implemented by several servers. Explain why resources might be transferred between them. Would it be satisfactory for clients to multicast all requests to the group of servers as a way of achieving mobility transparency for clients?

Q3. Summarize cloud standards.

Q4. List the main cloud security challenges.

Q5. Distinguish between clustering and replication.

Q6. Define the terms *cloud ecosystem, cloud sourcing, cloud analytics*, and *cloud governance*?

Q7. How are metering and billing done in the cloud?

Q8. What is virtualization? Give its advantages and disadvantages.

Q9. Define a VMM or hypervisor. Classify them.

Q10. Explain the two virtualization architectures in detail with clear and accurate diagrams. Give examples of both.

Q11. What is server virtualization? What are its different types?

Q12. Explain paravirtualization. Give its advantages and disadvantages.

Q13. What is cloud storage?

Q14. What is network virtualization? Explain it advantages.

Q15. What is application virtualization?

Q16. Why are Type-1 VMMs better than Type-2 VMMs?

Q17. Explain hardware emulation and OS virtualization.

Q18. What is MapReduce? Explain it briefly.

Q19. Explain the following:

(a) Cloud data centers

(b) Cisco network architectures

Q20. Why is cloud security a bigger challenge?

Q21. What is the amplification rule with respect to web application-based security?

[Hints: As discussed, in cloud computing environments, resources are provided as a service over the Internet in a dynamic, virtualized, and scalable way. Through cloud computing services, users access business applications online from a web browser. However, software and data are stored on the servers. The website server is the first gate that guards the vast cloud resources. Since the cloud may operate continuously to process millions of dollars of online transactions daily, the impact of any web security vulnerability will be amplified at the level of cloud computing.]

Q22. Discuss various technologies for data security in cloud computing. How is database sourcing important in the cloud?

Q23. How does encryption, digital signatures, PKI, and SSO help in cloud security?

Q24. How can you reduce cloud security breaches?

[Hints: The following steps may be followed:

1. Authenticate all users using the network.

2. Authenticate software running on any computer.

3. Formalize the process of requesting permission to access data or applications.

4. Monitor all network activity and log all unusual activity.

5. Analyze all log user activity for its unexpected behavior.

6. Do encryption of the entire data you use.

7. Do regular vulnerability scans of the network.]

Q25. Define a silo.

[Hint: A silo is an isolated piece of software and hardware that cannot interact with other components.]

Q26. Distinguish between static and dynamic virtualization.

[Hints: In static virtualization, application silos become virtualized application silos. On the other hand, to optimize a working environment, you should be able to allocate server resources dynamically, based on changing needs within the business. This is complex dynamic virtualization. It is inevitable because the workloads in the data center are dynamic.]

Q27. Explain the 11 security design principles.

Q28. What is a policy? What are its different types? Explain with examples.

Q29. Explain your understanding of cloud storage in detail.

Q30. Write short summaries on:

(a) Pre-cloud computing.

(b) Digital certificates.

(c) Web conferencing tools like Adobe Connect, Glance, WebEx, Zoho Meeting, Yugma, IBM Lotus Sametime.

(d) Cloud security services.

(e) SLAs.

CHAPTER 4

ADVANCED CLOUD APPLICATIONS

4.1 INTRODUCTION

D ue to the different features of the cloud such as multiple user access, unlimited storage, low expenditure, unlimited storage, and so on, clouds have many applications including big data analytics, development and testing, disaster recovery, games, and web and mobile applications. The range of applications is vast. The cloud collaborates with task management, web databases and social networks, and web services like emailing, blogs, and wikis.

4.2 SPECIALIZED CLOUD ARCHITECTURE

Cloud architecture should consist of two parts:

1. Front end (client-side)

2. Back end (cloud-side)

The *front end* means some applications and client devices through which the user can access the cloud computing system. All systems do not have the same GUIs. The right architecture selection for an application will further improve the cloud security.

The *back end* means only the part of the cloud that includes servers, systems, and storage systems that can be accessed by the users. It has web application programs like data processing, gaming, entertainment, and software development. Every application has its own server for services. For better management of the cloud, a central server must exist. This server will follow some protocols and use a special type of software called *middleware* that communicates with the users who are connected to the cloud server. This server manages traffic and reduces complexities. A diagram is shown in Figure 4.1.

FIGURE 4.1 Cloud architecture.

This type of cloud architecture has several advantages including a pay-per-use model, easy management, rapid development, and elasticity.

4.2.1 Direct I/O Access

As already mentioned, virtualization is a technique that is used to separate service requests and service delivery from each other. A special layer called a *virtualization layer* separates the hardware and operating system (OS) from each other in 8086 systems. This layer provides a logical mechanism to run multiple concurrent OSs on a single piece of hardware. To achieve this functionality, dynamic partitioning and resource sharing are carried out. These resources may be CPU, memory, storage, and I/O devices.

Other than CPU and memory virtualizations, I/O virtualization is also possible. It involves management of I/O request routing between virtual devices and the physical hardware being shared among them. For an effective virtualization of I/O, the CPU utilization is kept to a minimum whereby the advantages of virtualization are preserved.

Better features and simple management are possible in virtualization and management of the I/O using a hosted architecture. An example is networking where virtual networks are created between the guest systems by virtual NICs and switches.

4.2.2 Load-Balanced Virtual Switches

The cloud is elastic. This elasticity can be achieved by combining CloudWatch, autoscaling, and elastic load balancing features, which allow the number of instances to scale up and down automatically based on a set of customizable rules and traffic to be distributed across several instances. By default, fixed IP addresses or elastic IPs are not available, but you can pay more and get them. Elastic IP addresses allow you to allocate a static IP address. Thus, you can distribute incoming traffic by creating an elastic load balancer using an elastic load balancing service.

Even web requests are divided among servers during load balancing. Each request is taken in order and distributed to the next server in line. It may also be a weighted distribution. In such a case, some devices in the load-balanced array are capable of handling various load amounts. This reduces the amount of load on those servers.

In geographical load balancing, the geographic portion describes how the system is able to do a reverse lookup on source Internet addresses.

Load balancers can be used to manage and spread incoming user traffic among multiple servers. A load balancer monitors the traffic and available servers and uses a round-robin algorithm where the idle server is allocated the load. This improves performances as well and prevents server failures. If a server fails, the other servers continue to provide the services but may be slower. On a larger scale, a load balancer can distribute traffic to servers all around the world.

In summary, load balancers improve performance and availability. If a given site is down, the load balancer avoids the failed site and continues to service the users using servers in other regions. Load balancers are used for services like Domain Name System (DNS), HTTP, FTP, and so on. They are very useful for applications where the incoming load varies rapidly. They are also useful when connections are intelligent. They help by enabling an intelligent management interface to the application services.

4.2.3 Multipath Resource Access

As we know, the pay-per-use model for the cloud allows maximum resource utilization. However, minimal resource management is also necessary.

4.3 FEDERATED CLOUDS

The term *federation* means an integration of different smaller units encapsulated to do different tasks. A federation of clouds is the mechanism used by the cloud provider whereby it rents resources, applications, or services from various cloud vendors to meet exponential customer needs.

Advantages of Federated Clouds

Different applications and unlimited resources can be available from a single provider. The interaction between multi-vendor services is tested by the providers. There is no vendor lock-in because services come from different providers. Because resources are distributed through many providers, the utilization percentage is very high. This reduces the cost for consumers. The performance is better because caching is performed and also due to the fact that multiple data copies are available at different provider locations. These copies can be accessed by the users globally. Data availability is better in federated clouds because data is replicated to multiple sites. Security in multi-vendor federated clouds is another issue. However, the data is physically present in different cloud data centers (CDCs) all around the globe.

In federated clouds, customers must make sure that all cloud providers audit their environments. The customers must also follow the regulations. They must be knowledgeable about the security policies and should know about the SLA agreements with federated providers. A federated cloud needs a robust identity management system.

In federated cloud computing, two types of actors are identified as follows:

- **Service Providers (SPs)**: These are the entities that need computational resources to offer some services. However, they do not own these resources, rather they lease them from Infrastructure Providers (IPs).

- **Infrastructure Providers (IPs):** IPs provide SPs with a seemingly infinite pool of computational, network, and storage resources.

We define a service application as a set of software components that work collectively to achieve a common goal.

To create the illusion of an infinite pool of resources, infrastructure providers shared their unused capacity with each other to create a federation cloud. Thus, the benefits of federation-capable cloud computing need to be synthesized. Any federation of cloud computing providers should allow virtual applications to be deployed across federated sites.

Just as the Internet is a network of networks, a cloud federation enables an *intercloud* or a *cloud of clouds*. Just as we use the electrical grid on a shared basis, the intercloud is a mesh of cloud computing resources owned by multiple parties and interconnected and shared via open standards.

Cloud federation enables cloud service providers to:

1. Maximize profit by servicing more customers using existing infrastructure while still meeting SLAs by balancing loads across fellow service providers during demand spikes.

2. Obtain better revenue from existing customers by selling services on a large scale.

3. Derive more revenues from other service providers by renting them unused capacity on an as-needed basis.

Challenges of Cloud Federation

There are two main challenges in federated clouds:

1. **On the Operational Side:** It is not easy to migrate and then deploy VMs anywhere flexibly and rapidly.

2. **On the Cloud Federation Management Side:** Companies must find ways to dynamically coordinate service loads among cloud service providers. They must establish a common authentication scheme. Furthermore, cloud federations need better reconciliation and billing systems.

Cloud providers can solve these challenges on a case-by-case basis but some hard work is needed.

The main concept behind the intercloud is that each single cloud does not have infinite physical resources. If a cloud were saturated, the computational and storage resources would still be able to satisfy requests for service allocations sent from its clients. This is analogous to the Internet and also to the way mobile operators work on their roaming and inter-carrier interoperability. Identity management, security event management, and federation are all inter-related to each other. Cloud federation is a practice of interconnecting the cloud computing environments of two or more service providers to perform load balancing and to accommodate spikes in demand. It will become an important part of cloud computing services in the future.

Cloud federation requires one provider to wholesale or rent computing resources to another cloud provider. Those resources become a temporary or permanent extension of the buyer's cloud computing environment, depending on the specific federation agreement between providers. It provides two benefits to cloud providers as follows:

(a) It allows providers to earn revenue from computing resources that would otherwise be idle or underutilized.

(b) It enables cloud providers to expand their geographic footprints and accommodate sudden spikes in demand without having to build new points-of-presence (POPs).

Service providers strive to make all aspects of cloud federation ranging from cloud provisioning to billing support systems (BSS) and customer support, transparent to the customers. When a federating cloud services with a partner, cloud providers will also establish extensions of their customer-facing SLAs into their partner provider's data centers.

The cloud is a metaphor for the methods that enable users to access applications and services using the Internet and the web. Everything from the access layer to the bottom of the stack is located in the data center and never leaves it. Within this stack are many other applications and services that enable monitoring of the processing, memory, storage and network, which can then be used by the charge-back applications to provide metering and billing. This is a cloud federation stack.

As the cloud market increases and enlarges across the world, the diversity of provisioning is going to become increasingly difficult to manage. Many cloud providers could be hostile to each other and may not be keen to share across their clouds. Business and users will want to be able to diversify and multiply their choices of cloud delivery and provisioning. Having multiple clouds increases the availability of application and services.

4.4 BASICS OF CLOUD MOBILITY

According to Renaud Larsen, the Chief Architect for Cloud at Juniper Networks, "The mobile ecosystem has to traverse many complex layers, each of which adds network latency and transmission delay. In addition, the cloud allows users to swap devices and retain access to information—this is a disruptive development and means cloud apps need to cover the whole cross-device mobile infrastructure." Many companies find the integration of mobile and cloud very profitable as it cuts down the cost of developing and running mobile applications. Researchers say that (mobile + cloud) will promise green IT solutions in future.

The association of mobile computing and cloud services formed a new concept called *Mobile Cloud Computing* (MCC). It implies that MCC is the integration of the mobile computing environment with cloud computing services. Thus, now mobile users can have the full benefits of cloud computing technology. New services are now available on mobile devices. Several definitions of MCC have been given. Some of them are as follows:

> MCC refers to an infrastructure where both data storage and the data processing happen outside of the mobile device. Mobile cloud applications move the computing power and data storage away from the mobile phones and in the cloud, bringing applications and mobile computing to not just smartphone users but a much broader range of mobile subscribers. [MCC FORUM]

> "A model for enabling convenient, on-demand network access to a shared pool of configurable computing resources (like networks, servers storage, applications, and services) that can be rapidly provisioned and released with minimal management effort or service provider interaction." [NIST]

Figure 4.2 shows what an MCC looks like conceptually.

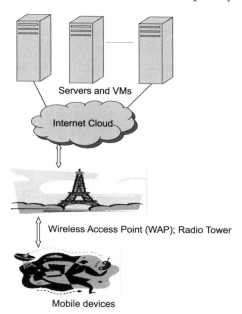

FIGURE 4.2 Mobile Cloud Computing [MCC] environment.

From Figure 4.2, it is clear that Virtual Machines (VMs) are provided on the cloud. They can be accessed by mobile devices through Wireless Access Points (WAPs). The MCC is a new model for mobile application users. They can use the powerful cloud platform, which uses centralized remote servers and other physical resources. Once in the cloud, mobile users can use their devices to access applications developed and deployed at a centralized location. For this, web browsers are used or a native thin client connected in wireless mode. This concept can be shown in an equation form as well:

MCC = Mobile Web Computing + Cloud Computing Services

Thus, cloud computing helps mobile users to access the applications and services available on the Internet. MCC is a technology that provides access to the best resources and applications by using mobile devices without requiring powerful configurations. Cloud services are able to handle complicated modules efficiently. Thus, users can now use more storage space and processing power. MCC provides many options to cloud providers, mobile users, application developers, and other stakeholders. The MCC architecture is very easy and is shown in Figure 4.3.

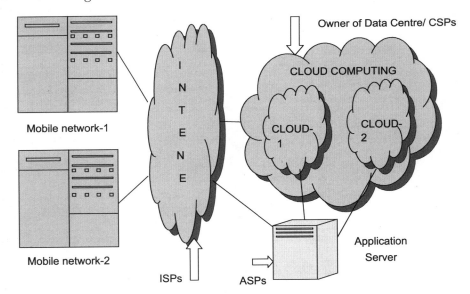

FIGURE 4.3 MCC architecture.

From Figure 4.3, it is clear that the cloud receives a request from the subscribers over the Internet. The requests made by mobile users are processed by the cloud controllers who then provide them with the requested cloud services. Utility computing, virtualization, and service-oriented architecture form the basis for the development of cloud services.

SUMMARY

In this chapter, we studied how the cloud has a very wide range of applications ranging from grid and parallel computing to mobile computing. Cloud computing provides certain services to the cloud. Even *mobile-as-a-service* is being investigated by researchers today. We saw in this chapter how these different networks and service providers work together to achieve cloud objectives. The concept is that of Software and Service (S + S). The S+S can perform a task in the cloud through a mobile device. There are many free applications that may be used on a cloud. For instance, Google's free apps let you work on documents on your laptop and then you can even work on that document on a mobile. About 334 companies are working together today to use S+S. The first deliverable in this regard was Android, which is a completely integrated mobile software stack that includes a middleware, an OS, and a better GUI.

CONCEPTUAL SHORT QUESTIONS WITH ANSWERS

Q1. What are the issues related to S + S?

Ans. 1 Cost, Quality of Service (QoS), and people's fear regarding cloud data security are some of its disadvantages.

Q2. What is MAaaS?

Ans. 2 MAaaS stands for Mobile Application as a Service, which allows the creation of people-centric applications across various domains. It is a cloud-based framework for storing, processing, and delivering data from mobile- sensing to people-centric applications.

Q3. What is a federated cloud?

Ans. 3 By the term *federation* we mean an integration of different smaller units encapsulated to do different tasks. A federation of clouds is the mechanism used by the cloud provider whereby it rents resources, applications, or services from various cloud vendors to meet exponential customer needs.

Q4. What are the advantages of federated clouds?

Ans. 4 Different applications and unlimited resources are available from a single provider. The interaction between the multi-vendor services is tested by the providers. There is no vendor lock-in because services come from different providers. Since the resources are distributed through many providers, the utilization percentage is very high. This reduces the cost for consumers. The performance is better because caching is done and also due to the fact that multiple data copies are available at different provider locations. These copies can be accessed by users globally. Data availability is better in federated clouds because data is replicated to multiple sites. Security in this multi-vendor federated cloud is another issue. However, the data is physically present in different cloud data centers (CDCs) all around the globe.

In federated clouds, customers must make sure that all cloud providers audit their environments. They must follow the regulations too. They must be knowledgeable about security policy and should know about SLA agreements with federated providers. A federated cloud needs a robust identity management system.

Q5. What is the main concept behind an intercloud?

Ans. 5 The main concept behind an intercloud is that each single cloud does not have infinite physical resources. If a cloud becomes saturated, the computational and storage resources would still be able to satisfy requests for service allocations sent from its clients. This is analogous to the Internet and also to the way mobile operators work with their roaming and inter-carrier interoperability. Identity management, security event management, and federation are all inter-related to each other.

CHAPTER REVIEW QUESTIONS

Q1. Name all the resources that are vulnerable to attacks by an unauthorized program, which can be downloaded from a remote site.

Q2. What are federated clouds? What are the challenges associated with them?

Q3. Explain S+S in the cloud.

Q4. What is MCC? Discuss its architecture. How are cloud and mobile integrated? Explain with clear diagrams.

Q5. What is a cast iron cloud?

[Hint: It was provided by IBM. Because data inconsistency is one of the major problems today, cast iron clouds provide consistent data from multiple resources, both on- and off-site. This results in a hybrid cloud solution. It comes in three packages: WebSphere Cast Iron Live, WebSphere Cast Iron Hypervisor Edition, and WebSphere DataPower Cast Iron XH40.]

CHAPTER 5

ENTERPRISE CLOUD COMPUTING

5.1 INTRODUCTION

Cloud computing is still in its infancy. Cloud providers bring evolution and revolution by introducing new services to the cloud. This is inescapable because customer requirements change frequently. Enterprises try to adjust the existing cloud models to best suit their needs. Enterprises will thus form new *Enterprise Cloud Paradigm Computing* models. Enterprise Cloud Computing (ECC) is the alignment of a cloud computing model with an organization's business objectives such as profit, ROI, reduction in operational costs, and processes. As per the NIST report, cloud computing has five main features: on-demand self-service, broad network access, resource pooling, rapid elasticity, and metered/measured service. Cloud stakeholders can deploy any of the models such as private clouds, public clouds, hybrid clouds, virtual private clouds, and community clouds. It is important to note that the selection of a deployment model depends on the opportunities to increase earnings and reduce costs—capital expenses (CAPEX) and operating expenses (OPEX). Additionally, the element of timeliness is also associated with cloud adoption. This means that the decisions that lead to losses today can be carried out with a vision toward increased earnings and cost reduction in the future.

5.2 DATA AND PROCESS

OLTP (Online Transaction Processing) is a transactional type of application. It refers to a class of systems that manage transaction-oriented applications like relational databases. These applications are based on four properties called *ACID properties*, Atomicity, Consistency, Isolation, and Durability. They are more write/update intensive applications. Applications like ERP, Sales Distributions, CRM, and SCM face many technical and non-technical challenges to deploy cloud environments. ACID properties are also difficult to guarantee given the concurrent cloud-based data management and storage systems. It is necessary to break highly complex enterprise applications into smaller functional components using a decomposition technique.

OLAP (Online Analytical Processing) is an application that is used to efficiently answer multi-dimensional queries for analysis, reporting, and decision support. Examples of OLAP applications include business reporting, marketing, budgeting, and forecasting. They all belong to a larger Business Intelligence (BI) category. These applications are mostly read-only and ACID guarantees are not required. It is important to understand that because of OLAP's data-intensive and data-parallel nature, this type of application can benefit greatly from the flexible compute and storage available on the cloud. Furthermore, BI and analytical applications are relatively better suited to run on a cloud platform with a shared-nothing architecture. Today, researchers say that Analytics-as-a-Service may be a new cloud service. The following points are worth noting:

1. Data sources residing within private or public clouds can be processed using flexible computing resources on-demand, which are accessible via APIs, web services, SQL, BI, and data mining tools.

2. Security, data integrity, and other issues cannot be overlooked, but the cloud offers a direction with unbelievable performance and total cost of ownership (TCO) as far as analytical processing is concerned.

In summary, analytical applications will benefit more than their transactional counterparts from the new opportunities opened by cloud computing. Since CRM and HR are functionally separate components today, they are also offered as hosted services.

Processes: To migrate an existing application or service to a public cloud, some steps must be followed. Larger enterprises have large-revenue impacted services and are bound to follow a more deliberate cloud application process. Their processes are often slower than they would prefer. They must evaluate:

- User requirements
- Cost-benefit analysis (CBA)

- Data migration issues

- Reuse of existing in-house hardware and applications

For enterprises, the adoption process of public clouds includes the following phases:

Phase-1: Assessment

Phase-2: Proof of Concept (PoC)

Phase-3: Pilot Migration

Phase-4: Testing

Phase-5: Go-Live

Phase-6: Audit

The Assessment phase includes:

- Data criticality assessment

- Cloud provider functionality

- Security

- SLA

- Features assessment

- Estimated CBA

The PoC phase includes a vendor evaluation to make sure that vendors have the required functionality. The enterprise IT manager or administrator receives login access to run through the cloud features.

The Pilot Migration phase includes:

- Migration of a few users to the cloud

- Benefit analysis

- Data migration

The Testing phase includes:

- User acceptance testing

- Actual be nefit analysis

- ROI
- Issues and risks
- Enterprise migration of user data to the cloud and testing of the application
- Security testing
- Service uptime

The Go-Live phase includes:

- Phased deployment
- User training
- User documentation and operating procedures
- User acceptance testing

5.3 ENTERPRISE CLOUD CONSUMPTION STRATEGIES

There are four cloud consumption strategies as follows:

1. **Software Provision:** The cloud provides software instances but the data is maintained within the user's data center.

2. **Storage Provision:** The cloud provides data management and software access to data remotely from the user's data center.

3. **Solution Provision:** Software and storage are maintained in the cloud and the user does not maintain the data center.

4. **Redundancy Services:** The cloud is used as an alternative or extension of the user's data center for software and storage.

NOTE

These consumption strategies make a distinction between data and application logic because issues such as programming models used, data sensitivity, software licensing, and expected response times must be considered.

5.4 ENTERPRISE CLOUD ADOPTION STRATEGIES

There are four main enterprise cloud adoption strategies using basic cloud drivers as follows:

1. **Scalability-driven strategy:** Use of cloud resources to support additional load or as backup.

2. **Availability-driven strategy:** Use of load balanced and localized cloud resources to increase availability and reduce response time.

3. **Market-driven strategy:** Users and providers of cloud resources make decisions based on the potential savings and profit.

4. **Convenience-driven strategy:** Using cloud resources so that there is no need to maintain local resources.

5.5 APPLICATION ENTERPRISE SOFTWARE—ERP, SCM, AND CRM

ERP (Enterprise Resource Planning) describes enterprise applications today. The purpose of ERP solutions is to equip enterprises with a tool to optimize their underlying business processes. ERP solutions have emerged as the core of successful information management and the enterprise backbone. Al-Mashari et al. report that adequate IT infrastructure, hardware, and networks are crucial for an ERP system to be successful. ERP implementation involves a complex transition from legacy information systems and business processes to an integrated IT infrastructure and common business process throughout an organization. Hardware selection is driven by the choice of ERP software package by an organization. IaaS has better future scenarios for ERP implementation.

OLTP (Online Transaction Processing) is a transactional type of application. It refers to a class of systems that manage transaction-oriented applications like relational databases. As we know, these applications are based on four properties called *ACID properties*: Atomicity, Consistency, Isolation, and Durability. They are more write/update intensive applications. Applications like ERP, sales distributions, CRM, and SCM face many technical and non-technical challenges to deploy cloud environments. ACID properties are also difficult to guarantee given the concurrent cloud-based data management and storage systems. It is necessary to break highly complex enterprise applications into smaller functional components using a decomposition technique.

OLAP (Online Analytical Processing) are applications that are used to efficiently answer multi-dimensional queries for analysis, reporting, and decision support. Examples of OLAP applications include business reporting, marketing, budgeting, and forecasting. They all belong to a larger Business Intelligence (BI) category. These applications are mostly read-only and ACID guarantees are not required. It is important to understand that because of its data-intensive and data-parallel nature, this type of application can benefit largely from the flexible compute and storage available in the cloud. Furthermore, BI and analytical applications are relatively better suited to run on a cloud platform with a shared-nothing architecture. Currently, researchers report that Analytics-as-a-Service may be a new cloud service.

For example, salesforce.com focuses on CRM-related applications and provides both hosted software and a development platform.

SUMMARY

In this chapter, we studied the enterprise cloud computing model/paradigm with respect to opportunities, challenges, and strategies for cloud adoption and consumption. As per the Gartner report of 2008, enterprise cloud computing is in its first phase called *inflated expectation*. In the next ten years, ECC will flourish. We have seen in this chapter that ECC aims at alignment of the cloud computing model within an organization's businesses and processes. We also studied issues such as which deployment model to select, strategies for ECC, issues related to ECC, ECC stakeholders using clouds, and so on.

CONCEPTUAL SHORT QUESTIONS WITH ANSWERS

Q1. Telenor uses MS Azure VM for testing of the company-wide SharePoint 2013 platform. What potential benefits has Telenor obtained by moving to the cloud?

Ans. 1 By utilizing MS Azure VM, Telenor has dramatically reduced the costs needed for test, development and demo environments, reduced the time to make the environments available to the project, and saved on long-term investment in hardware that would have only been used in the short term.

Q2. Explain Porter's model. What do the elements signify?

Ans. 2 Porter described a framework for industry analysis and business strategy development. He classified actors, products, and business models.

Porter's model is given in Figure 5.1:

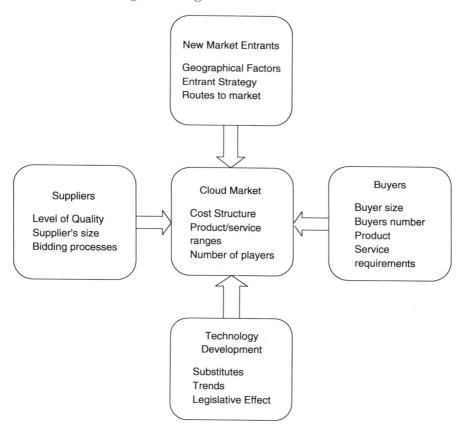

FIGURE 5.1 Porter's 5 Forces Market model.

Explanation: The number of companies that are dealing with cloud and virtualization is very high today. Yet, this might cause problems in the future because exponential rise is always difficult to handle. The battle for customers and struggle for market share will begin when the market becomes saturated. In addition, the preliminary costs for CDCs (Cloud Data Centers) are also very high. When a customer can easily switch from one product to another, then the frenzy to get more and more customers also increases. On the other hand, high exit barriers discourage customers from buying new technology. Thus, the trend is to standardize formats and architectures.

Q3. Summarize the cloud supply chain.

Ans. 3 The complexity of deploying, securing, interconnecting, and maintaining enterprise landscapes and solutions like ERP will be considered in the future. The concept of a cloud supply chain (C-SC) and therefore Cloud Supply Chain Management (C-SCM) appears to be a feasible solution for ECC. The idea of C-SCM represents the management of a network of interconnected businesses involved in the end-to-end provision of a product required by the customers. Thus, we can define C-SC more formally as "two or more parties linked by the provision of cloud services, related information, and funds."

Q4. What are the two cloud pricing models today?

Ans. 4 Two types of cloud pricing models are as follows:

(a) **Allocation-based:** This works on the principle of allocation of resources for a fixed amount of time; for example, like Amazon.

(b) **Usage-based:** This requires no reservation of resources and the cloud would simply allocate resources on a per-need basis.

Q5. The very concept of the cloud represents a leap from the traditional approach for IT to deliver mission critical services. What transition challenges are faced during these transitions?

Ans. 5 The following challenges are faced:

1. Companies must understand their own IT assets and what is ready for the cloud.

2. Migration of existing or legacy/old applications to the cloud.

3. Because migration to the cloud depends on the concept of decoupling of processes, work needs to be organized using a process- or service-centric model. In addition, not all applications will be able to handle such migration without a complex re-engineering process.

4. Data security is another challenge.

5. It can be extrapolated that SOA underlies the architecture and the operation of the enterprise cloud.

6. Challenges are of two types, running the enterprise cloud and running applications on the enterprise cloud.

CHAPTER REVIEW QUESTIONS

Q1. The adoption process of public clouds by enterprises includes various phases. Name them and explain them.

Q2. What is ECC? What challenges do you face when deploying ECC?

Q3. What are enterprise cloud consumption strategies?

Q4. What are enterprise cloud adoption strategies?

Q5. Explain application enterprise software. Explain ERP, SCM, and CRM and their conjunction with cloud computing?

CHAPTER 6

CASE STUDIES

6.1 INTRODUCTION

C loud collaboration using different software applications available on the net for sharing of data and information is becoming essential today. The term *collaboration* refers to a complex task that allows multiple persons located remotely (far away) to work in real time on different types of tasks using web-related applications. Several large web companies like Amazon and Google now claim that they have data storage capacity that can be rented out to others. This process is known as *cloud storage*. This means that data that is stored far away can now be cached onto your PCs, tablets, mobile devices, or any other device on the Internet. Examples include Amazon Elastic Compute Cloud (EC2) and Simple Storage Solution (S3).

6.2 OPEN SOURCE, COMMONLY AVAILABLE TOOLS, AND PLATFORMS

Cloud computing includes a complete set of computing stacks from hardware architecture to end-user programming applications; for example, Amazon is the chief player in providing its solution (AWS) in IaaS in public clouds. In addition, by applying the MS Azure SDK, developers can build services that control the .net framework. At the microscopic level, VM technologies like Xen, KVM, and VMware aid in developing virtual infrastructures. Virtual machine managers,

VMware vCloud, and Eucalyptus (discussed in Section 6.8), allow the supervision of a virtual infrastructure and making a cluster or a grid into a private cloud. In the case of PaaS, we see DataSynapse, Elastra, Zimory Pools, and AppLogic.

Open Nebula's architecture is modular in design so it is easy to integrate it with any virtualization platform in the cloud ecosystem that includes cloud toolkits, service managers, virtual image managers, and also VM schedulers like Haizea. Haizea is a storage rental manager. By combining Open Nebula and Haizea, a virtual management infrastructure can be formed.

Similarly, OpenPEX allows users to provision resources in advance. Similar to Zimory, Aneka is characterized by a programming agent that can be set on physical and virtual resources. This will form a runtime environment in the cloud. It harnesses the computing resources of a heterogeneous network of workstations and servers or data centers on demand. Aneka provides developers with a rich set of APIs for programming. System administrators can use a collection of tools to monitor, manage, and control the deployed infrastructure. Such an infrastructure can be a public cloud available to everyone on the Internet, a private cloud having a set of nodes with restricted access, or a hybrid cloud where external resources are integrated through an on-demand basis. This allows applications to scale well.

Aneka is an implementation of the PaaS model. It provides a runtime environment for executing applications. Developers can express distributed applications by using APIs contained in the SDK or by porting existing legacy applications to the cloud. Such applications are executed on the Aneka cloud, represented by a collection of nodes connected through the network hosting Aneka container. The container is a building block of the middleware.

CometCloud is an autonomic computing engine for cloud and grid environments. It is based on the Comet decentralized coordination substrate. It supports highly heterogeneous and dynamic cloud infrastructures, integration of public/private clouds, and autonomic cloud bursts. It is based on a peer-to-peer substrate that can span data centers, grids and clouds. Resources can be obtained on demand and on-the-fly into its peer-to-peer overlay to provide services to applications.

Combining public cloud platforms and integrating them with existing grids and data centers supports on-demand scale-up, scale-down, and scale-out. CometCloud is an autonomic cloud engine. The objective is to realize a virtual computational cloud with resizable computing capability that integrates local computational environments and public cloud services on demand. In addition, cloud computing enables policy-based autonomic cloud bridging and cloud bursting.

Autonomic cloud bridging enables on-the-fly integration of local computational environments (data centers, grids) and public cloud services like Amazon EC2 and Eucalyptus.

Autonomic cloud bursting enables dynamic application scale-out to address dynamic workloads, spikes in demand, and other extreme requirements.

6.3 MS AZURE

This is Microsoft's cloud-based application platform for building, deploying, and managing applications off-site and providing services through a global network by Microsoft managed data centers. It provides both PaaS and IaaS services and supports many different programming languages, tools, and frameworks, including both MS-specific and third-party software and systems. Azure was released on February 1, 2010. It is an Internet-scale computing and service platform hosted in data centers managed or supported by MS. It includes many separate features with corresponding developer services that can be used individually or together. One drive is MS Cloud Storage with a positioning line of "One Place for Everything in your Life." One can easily store and share photos, videos, documents, et cetera, anywhere, on any device for free. In addition, you get 7GB when you sign up.

For example, Toyota Motor Corporation Ltd. has 16 websites that deliver more than 100 million page views per month. The company's site provides vital information to its car owners including vehicle information, social networking, news, and entertainment. To enhance site content, increase scalability, and reduce the cost of ownership, Toyota is rebuilding the site using the MS Azure cloud development environment and MS SharePoint 2013.

When you deploy your application and services to the cloud, Azure provides the necessary virtual machines, network bandwidth, and other infrastructure resources. Should machines go down for hardware updates or because of unexpected failures, Azure locates new virtual machines for your application automatically. In addition, Azure provides automatic infrastructure services.

MS Azure allows you to easily adjust your resource utilization to match the load. Dynamic scaling is defined as the capability to both scale out and scale back your application depending on the resource requirements. This feature is also called *elastic scaling*. Actually, with cloud services you create roles that work together to implement your application logic. For example, one web role could host the ASP.NET front end of your application. One or more worker roles could perform the vital background tasks. One or more virtual machines hosting each role are called *role instances* in the MS Azure data center. In addition, requests are load balanced across these instances. This means that in this situation, as resource demands increase, you can provision new role instances to handle the load. When demand decreases, you can remove these instances so that you do not have to pay for unnecessary computing power. Furthermore, there are options for automatically scaling up and down based on predefined rules and policies.

MS Azure provides a platform for applications that can reliably store and access server data through storage services or the MS Azure SQL Database.

MS Azure ensures high availability of compute resources. For websites, you can meet the requirements of the Service Level Agreement (SLA) with only a single instance, whereas for cloud services and VMs, you can meet the SLA requirements by having at least two (2) instances per role or machine type. For VMs, the instances must be interchangeable, load balanced, and part of the availability group. However, in both cases, MS Azure monitors the actual hardware that hosts these VMs and instances. MS Azure is able to respond quickly to hardware restarts or failures by deploying new instances or moving application code and processing to other working hardware. In addition, MS Azure ensures high availability and durability for data stored by one of its storage services. MS Azure storage replicates all data to at least three different servers. By default, this storage also replicates to a secondary MS Azure region. Similarly, the MS Azure SQL Database replicates all data to promise its availability and durability.

MS Azure is very well suited for hosting highly available services.

Case Study 1: Consider an online shopping store that is deployed in MS Azure. As we know, this online store is a revenue generator, so it is very important that it stays up and running. To achieve this objective, the MS Azure data center performs service monitoring and automatic instance management. The online store must stay responsive to customer's demands. It is the elastic scaling ability of MS Azure that does this task. During peak shopping hours, new instances can come online to handle the increased usage. The orders must not be lost. Both MS Azure and the Azure SQL Database provide highly available and durable storage options to hold the order details and stay throughout the order life cycle. For the highest levels of availability, you can deploy the same application to multiple MS Azure regions. It is also possible to design a service that remains available even if an entire MS Azure region experiences a temporary failure. Doing this requires proper synchronization architecture and procedures for routing users.

Case Study 2: Consider a demo utility application that you want to make available only for several days or weeks. Such applications need not run continuously. MS Azure allows you to easily create, deploy, and share that application with the world. Once its purpose is accomplished, you can remove the application and you are only charged for the time it was deployed.

Case Study 3: Consider a large company (KR & R Company) that runs complex data analysis of sales numbers at the end of each month. It is a processing-intensive application because the total time required to complete the analysis is at most two days. In an on-premises scenario, the server required for this work would be underutilized for the majority of the month. However, in MS Azure, the business would pay only for the time that the analysis application is running in the cloud. Furthermore, assume that the architecture of the application is designed for parallel processing. The scale-out features of MS Azure would allow the company to create a large number of worker role instances or VMs. Thus, working together they can complete work that is more complex in less time.

Case Study 4: Consider a sports portal (a small website) that makes money from advertising. Here, the amount of revenue is directly proportional to the amount of traffic that the site generates. The company does not have money to set up and run its own data center. By designing the website to run on MS Azure, the company can easily deploy its solution as an ASP.NET application. The application will use an MS Azure SQL Database for relational data and blob storage for animations.

If the popularity of the website grows dramatically, the company can increase the number of web role instances for its front end. The company can also increase the size of the MS Azure SQL Database. The blob storage has built-in scalability features with MS Azure.

If the business decreases, the company can remove any unnecessary instances. Because its revenue is proportional to the traffic on the site, MS Azure helps the company to start small, grow fast, and reduce the risks.

With MS Azure you have complete control to determine how to manage your computing costs. Automatic scaling can also be done through the use of the Autoscale feature, which can add and remove instances based on rules. You could vary the number of instances also based on the predetermined amount.

For example, you might have two instances during business hours and one instance during non-business hours. You could also keep the number of instances constant and increase them only through the web portal manually as the demand increases over time. MS Azure gives you such flexibility.

Imagine that on this sports portal as the business grows slowly, some sort of temporary spikes or bursts of activity are observed. This may be due to the fact that another popular news website wants to refer to this site thereby increasing the number of visitors per day. This case is also a true candidate for elastic scaling and deployment because the process is active a few hours each day. MS Azure is well suited for temporarily scaling out an application to handle load spikes and then scaling back after the event has passed.

Even applications with steady workload patterns achieve cost savings using MS Azure. It is difficult to manage your own data centers because they are expensive, including the cost of energy, people, skills, hardware, software licensing, and facilities. However, MS Azure will reduce the total costs and will make costs clear too.

MS Azure VMs and the virtual network simplify the task of migration of on-premises servers and networks to the cloud. It is MS Azure that is now responsible for providing the required computing and storage resources for those applications.

MS Azure provides a pricing calculator for understanding specific costs. It also provides a TCO Calculator that estimates the overall cost reduction that a company would achieve by adopting MS Azure.

In summary, there are three major options on MS Azure to run applications:

(a) MS Azure Web Sites

(b) MS Azure Cloud Services

(c) MS Azure Virtual Machines Cloud Supply Chain Management (C-SCM)

Additionally, the websites and cloud services are both PaaS offerings where MS Azure provides all of the hardware and OS images while the developer provides the application code that runs on the platform. VMs provide IaaS offerings, which means that you manage machine images that run inside MS Azure data centers. MS Azure can be leveraged for a range of scenarios to ensure the highest levels of availability, managing unpredictable growth, and handling workload spikes.

MS wants to focus on devices and services at the same time. The term *devices* means devices of different shapes and sizes (and not smartphones or tablets). Similarly, *services* would include the cloud to keep these devices connected and the services those devices consume.

6.4 GOOGLE APP ENGINE

Try to visit the Google App Engine website at http://code.google.com/appengine. You will find four features listed:

(a) No assembly required.

(b) Google App Engine exposes a fully integrated development environment.

(c) It is easy to scale.

(d) It is free to get started.

These four features illustrate Google's strategy for PaaS. The aim is not to create every application to run on every platform but to help customers develop web-based applications. The platform is for development and deployment. Google provides accounts for authentication, the Google native file system called *GFS* (Google File System), and the Bigtable platform for data management, that is, a distributed storage system that manages very large-scale structured data.

Google has integrated all development tools into a single integrated environment. When customers combine their development with the Google life cycle, they also gain access to Google's IaaS. In this way, customers can add more capacity on demand.

Google also includes infrastructure services like load balancing, persistent storage queries, sorting and transactions, programming interfaces to support authenticating users, sending email using Google Accounts, and scheduling tasks for triggering events at specified times and regular intervals.

NOTE *This is the same platform that Google uses to build its own software.*

Google App Engine is a PaaS cloud that provides a complete web service environment, that is, all the required hardware, OS, and software are provided to the clients. According to Google, "Google App Engine lets you run web applications on Google's infrastructure. App Engine applications are easy to build, easy to maintain and easy to scale as your traffic and data storage needs grow. With App Engine, there are no servers to maintain: You just upload your application and it is ready to serve your users." The purpose is to divorce you from OS-dependent issues and provide native Python and JVM (Java Virtual Machine) support. You can leverage the amazing amount of free resources available to anyone. The SDK download is available for Mac, Windows, and Linux.

With the App Engine's Java runtime environment, you can build your app using standard Java technologies like JVM, Java Servlets, and the Java programming languages or any other language using a JVM-based interpreter or compiler like Ruby or JavaScript. With the App Engine's dedicated Python runtime environment, you have access to a fast Python interpreter and the Python standard library.

The Java and Python runtime environments are built to ensure that your application runs quickly, securely, and without interference from other apps on the system. With the App Engine, you only pay for what you use. There are no set-up costs and no recurring fees. The resources your application uses like storage and bandwidth are measured by the gigabyte. The App Engine costs nothing to start. All applications can use up to 500 MB of storage and enough CPU and bandwidth to support an efficient app serving around 5 million page views a month, free. In addition, for a better web development environment, the App Engine system has a tightly integrated database with an Imaging API, Mail API, and MemCache to handle CDNs.

Google App Engine integrates the following tools:

1. Python runtime.

2. Java runtime.

3. **Software Development Kit (SDK):** Enables developers to write application code.

4. **Web-based Administration Console:** Helps developers manage their applications.

5. **A Datastore:** A software layer that stores a web application's data.

6.5 AMAZON WEB SERVICES (AWS)

AWS, that is, Amazon Web Service offers a variety of cloud services including:

- S3 (storage).

- EC2 (virtual servers).

- Cloudfront (content delivery).

- Cloudfront Streaming (video streaming).

- SimpleDB (structured datastore).

- RDS (relational database).

- SQS (reliable messaging).

- Elastic MapReduce (data processing).

- The Elastic Compute Cloud (EC2) offers XEN-based virtual servers (instances) that can be instantiated from Amazon Machine Images (AMIs).

- These instances are available in different sizes, OSs, architectures, and price.

- CPU capacity of instances is measured in Amazon compute units. They vary among instance types from 1 (small instance) to 20 (high CPU instance).

- Each instance provides a certain amount of non-persistent disk space. A persistence disk service (Elastic Block Storage) allows attaching virtual disks to instances with space for up to 1TB.

- Elasticity can be achieved by combining the CloudWatch, Autoscaling, and Elastic Load Balancing features. This allows the number of instances to scale up and down automatically based on a set of customizable rules and traffic to be distributed across available instances.

- A fixed IP address (elastic IPs) is not available by default but can be obtained for an additional cost.

6.6 HADOOP

As per the IDC report, the size of the digital universe is estimated at 0.18 zettabyte in 2006 and is forecasted to grow tenfold by 2011 to 1.8 zettabytes. A zettabyte is 1021 bytes or equivalently, one thousand exabytes, one million petabytes, or one billion terabytes. This is roughly of the same order of magnitude as one disk drive for every person in the world. This flood of data originates from different sources as follows:

1. The New York Stock Exchange generates about one terabyte of new trade data per day.

2. Facebook hosts approximately 10 billion photos, taking one petabyte of storage.

3. Ancestry.com, the genealogy site, stores around 2.5 petabytes of data.

4. The Internet Archive stores around 2 petabytes of data and is growing at a rate of 20 terabytes per month.

5. The Large Hadron Collider near Geneva, Switzerland will produce about 15 petabytes of data per year.

MS Research's MyLifeBits project gives a glimpse into the archiving of personal information that may become commonplace in the future. MyLifeBits was an experiment where an individual's interactions—phone calls, emails, and documents—were captured electronically and stored. The data gathered included a photo taken every minute, which resulted in an overall data volume of 1GB/ month. Even if the storage costs come down, the data volume for a future MyLifeBits service will be many times that.

It has been said that more data usually beats better algorithms. The upside is that big data is here. The downside is that we are struggling to store and analyze it. The problem today is that although the storage capacities of hard drives have increased massively over the years, access speeds have not kept up with that pace. Thus, some problems/issues need to be solved:

1. Increases in the probabilities of hardware failure.

2. Analysis must be able to combine the data in some way, that is, data read from one disk may need to be combined with data from any of another 99 disks.

Hadoop is a Java-based programming framework. It processes large sets of data on clusters of servers. It is part of the Apache project. The Hadoop framework is mainly used by giants like Google, IBM, and Yahoo. Windows and Linux support the Hadoop framework. It also works well with BSD and OSX. Hadoop is a very common technology that has been used for big data. It was created by Doug Cutting, the creator of Apache Lucene, the widely used text search library.

The following points characterize Hadoop:

1. Hadoop is written in Java and Java programs can run on any platform.

2. There is better fault tolerance with Hadoop because if one node fails on the Hadoop environment, there is no problem because it replicates and distributes the data efficiently and effectively over multiple nodes.

3. In the Hadoop framework, the server does not have to be very powerful. Less expensive servers may be chosen by the users to make them to work as Hadoop individual nodes.

4. At a minimum, a Hadoop network may use only two servers but it is also possible to scale these servers to thousands with minimal effort.

5. Every server in the framework provides a local computation and storage.

6. To execute a query, it splits it across many servers and finally the results of these sub-queries are integrated as a whole (to get a complete solution).

7. Hadoop has two main components:

   (a) Hadoop Distributed File System.

   (b) Hadoop MapReduce.

8. Google MapReduce and Hadoop MapReduce are two different implementations of the MapReduce concept. Both work on huge data sets so they need to depend on distributed file systems. Hadoop will make use of the HDFS (Hadoop Distributed File System) while Google MapReduce will use the GFS (Google File System). Furthermore, Hadoop is implemented in Java while Google MapReduce is in C++. Google uses its MapReduce framework to process 20 petabytes of data per day. The MapReduce system runs on top of the Google File System (GFS), within which data is loaded, partitioned into chunks, and each

chunk is replicated. The open source Hadoop was developed by Yahoo where it processes hundreds of terabytes of data on at least 10,000 cores.

9. Researchers are starting to study the MapReduce model for a better fit in the cloud.

10. Hadoop is a collection of related sub-projects that fall under the umbrella of infrastructure for distributed computing. Although Hadoop is best known for its MapReduce and HDFS, the other components of the sub-projects also play an important role. These include Core, Avro, MapReduce, HDFS, Pig, HBase, ZooKeeper, Hive, and Chukwa.

6.7 MAP REDUCE (MR)

MapReduce (MR) is a programming model for data processing. Hadoop can run MapReduce programs that are written in different programming languages. MR programs are inherently parallel. The approach taken by MapReduce seems like a brute force approach.

The premise is that the entire data set, or at least a good portion of it, is processed for each query. We define MapReduce as a batch query processor, which has the ability to run an ad hoc query against your whole data set and get the results within a reasonable time and it is transformative. It changes the way the data is stored on tape or disk. It provides users with an opportunity to innovate with data. For example, Mailtrust, Rackspace's mail division, uses Hadoop for processing email logs. One ad hoc query that they wrote was, "to find the geographic distribution of their users." The data was so useful that there are schedules for the MapReduce job to run monthly and the data will be used to help decide which Rackspace data centers to place new mailservers in as the company grows.

By bringing several hundred gigabytes of data together and having the tools to analyze it, the Rackspace engineers were able to gain an understanding of the data that they otherwise would have never had. They were able to use what they had learned to improve the service for their customers.

The question then becomes: Why can't we use databases with many disks? Why is MapReduce needed?

The answer is simple. The current trend is that disk seek time is improving more slowly than the transfer rate. We already know that seek time is the process of moving the disk's head to a specific place on the disk to read or write data while the transfer rate corresponds to a disk's bandwidth. If the data access pattern is dominated by seeks, then it will take longer to read or write large portions of a data set than streaming through it, which operates at the transfer rate. On the other hand, to update a small portion of records in a database, a traditional B-Tree works well. To update a good portion of a database, a B-Tree is less efficient than MapReduce, which uses sort/merge to rebuild the database. In many ways, MapReduce can be seen as a complement to an RDBMS. Table 6.1 compares a traditional RDBMS and MapReduce.

TABLE 6.1 RDBMS versus MapReduce

Traditional RDBMS	MapReduce
1. It can store up to gigabytes.	1. It can store up to petabytes.
2. It is interactive and has batch access.	2. It has batch access.
3. Read and write are done many times.	3. Write once, read many times.
4. It has a static schema.	4. It has a dynamic schema.
5. Higher integrity.	5. Lower integrity.
6. Non-linear scaling can be done.	6. Linear scaling is possible using a map function and a reduce function.
7. It works on structured data.	7. It works on unstructured or semi-structured data because it is designed to interpret data at processing time.
8. Normalization can be easily done here on relations and tables.	8. Normalization is difficult to achieve because it makes reading a record a non-local operation.
9. These include database tables with a predetermined format.	9. An example is a web server log, which is not normalized and is a good candidate for analysis with MapReduce.

From Table 6.1, it is clear that MapReduce is a good fit for problems that need to analyze the whole data set (in a batch fashion) specifically for ad hoc analysis. On the other hand, an RDBMS is good for point queries or updates where the data set has been indexed to deliver low latency retrieval and update times for a relatively small amount of data. MapReduce suits applications where the data is written once and read many times whereas a relational DBMS is good for data sets that are regularly updated.

MR (MapReduce) is an example of PaaS. The MR (MapReduce) framework allows users to do two things as follows:

(a) Define their own specific map and reduce algorithms.

(b) Utilize the respective PaaS infrastructure with its MR supporting usage modes such as elasticity, communications, and so on.

MapReduce (MR) has several features like simplicity, fault tolerance, and scalability. It is the most powerful realization of data-intensive cloud computing programming. MapReduce is a software framework for solving many large-scale computing problems. It uses two functions **Map()** and **Reduce()** that are commonly used in the LISP language (List Processing). The MapReduce system uses these two functions as follows:

(a) **The map function:** Written by the user and processes a key/value pair to generate a set of intermediate key/value pairs as follows:

map (key1, value1) → list (key2, value2)

(b) **The reduce function:** Also written by the user and merges all intermediate values associated with the same intermediate key as follows:

reduce (key2, list(value2)) → list (value2)

The following points characterize MapReduce:

1. It is very scalable.

2. It executes jobs batch-wise on priority.

3. Each job executes or fails in execution independently and then restarts also automatically.

4. More servers can also be added to improve scalability.

5. It is more flexible.

6. It is a parallel programming model that retrieves data from the Hadoop cluster.

7. The name itself, *MapReduce*, has two tasks associated with it. The map task and the reduce task. The map task takes a set of data and transforms it into another set of data in which the individual elements are split into tuples, that is, key/value pairs mentioned earlier. It processes tasks in parallel. The reduce task will take the input as the output of the map

task and then combines those tuples into smaller sets of data tuples. Note that the reduce function is executed only after the map task.

8. The MapReduce framework is responsible for task scheduling and task monitoring and also task re-executing if any task fails.

9. The MapReduce framework includes a single master called as *JobTracker* (to schedule and monitor jobs) and one slave known as the *TaskTracker* per cluster-node to execute the tasks (as per the directions from its master).

10. The entire MapReduce job is delayed if one TaskTracker becomes slower and then everything will end up waiting for the slowest task.

Applications for MapReduce (MR)

1. Inverted index construction

2. Document clustering

3. Web link graph traversal

The map() and reduce() functions are described in more detail in Section 3.12 in Chapter 3.

6.8 EUCALYPTUS

Eucalyptus is open source software that implements an Amazon Web Services compatible cloud, which is cost effective, flexible, and secure. It can be easily deployed in existing IT infrastructures to enjoy the benefits of both public and private cloud models. Eucalyptus is an acronym for "Elastic Utility Computing Architecture for Linking Your Programs to Useful Systems." Basically, Eucalyptus provides Infrastructure-as-a-Service (IaaS) offerings. The main advantage is that it provides easy and secure deployment. The private cloud is deployed on the premises of an enterprise and can be accessed by users over the intranet, so critical and important data remains secure from outside intrusion. It also provides AWS APIs. At any time, consumers can easily migrate or load balance their less sensitive data into the Amazon public cloud. Thus, they do not have to worry about the elasticity of their network.

Eucalyptus is free and open source software for building AWS-compatible private and hybrid cloud computing environments marketed by the company

Eucalyptus Systems. Eucalyptus enables pooling to provide compute, storage, and network resources that can be dynamically scaled up or down as the application workloads change. For example, you can build a self-serviced private cloud on the existing IT infrastructure of your company behind the firewall you have installed. This self-serviced private cloud enables the IaaS by an abstraction of three heterogeneous resources, that is, the computer, network, and storage.

History of Eucalyptus

Development of Eucalyptus began as a research project in the U.S.-based Rice University in 2003. In 2009, a company named *Eucalyptus Systems* was formed to commercialize the Eucalyptus software. Later in 2012, the firm entered into an agreement with AWS to maintain compatibility and API support. In 2014, it was acquired by HP (Hewlett-Packard), which incidentally has its own cloud offerings under the HPE Helion banner. The Helion portfolio has a variety of cloud-related products, which includes HP's own flavor of OpenStack called *HP Helion OpenStack*. Now Eucalyptus is a part of the HPE portfolio and is called *HPE Helion Eucalyptus*. It provides an open solution for building a hybrid cloud, leveraging the benefits of other HP Helion products.

Eucalyptus Terminology

Users can easily migrate instances from Eucalyptus to Amazon Elastic Cloud. Compute, storage, and network is managed only by the virtualization layer. Instances are separated by hardware virtualization. The following terminology is used by Eucalyptus:

1. **Images:** Any software module, configuration, application software, or system software bundled and deployed in the Eucalyptus cloud is called a *Eucalyptus Machine Image* (EMI).

2. **Instances:** When we run the image and use it, it becomes an instance. The controller will decide how much memory to allocate and provide all other resources.

3. **Networking:** The Eucalyptus network is divided into three modes:

   (a) **Managed Mode:** In this mode, it just manages a local network of instances, which includes security groups and IP addresses.

   (b) **System Mode:** In this mode, it assigns a MAC address and attaches the instance's network interface to the physical network through the NC's bridge.

(c) **Static Mode:** In this mode, it assigns IP addresses to instances.

NOTE *Static and system mode do not assign elastic IPs, security groups, or VM isolation.*

4. **Access Control:** It is used to provide restriction to users. Each user will get a unique identity. All identities can be grouped and managed by access control.

5. **Eucalyptus Elastic Block Storage (EBS):** It provides block-level storage volumes, which we attach to an instance.

6. **Autoscaling and Load Balancing:** This is used to automatically create or destroy instances or services based on requirements. **CloudWatch** provides different metrics for measurement.

7. **Euca2ool:** Euca2ool is the Eucalyptus CLI for interacting with web services. It is a Python-based tool, which is compatible with all the AWS services like S3, autoscaling, ELB (Elastic Load Balancing), CloudWatch, EC2, and so on. It is an all-in-one solution for both the AWS and Eucalyptus platforms.

8. Many other tools also exist that can be used to interact with Eucalyptus and AWS and they are as follows:

    (a) **S3curl:** This is a tool for interaction between Eucalyptus Walrus and AWS S3.

    (b) **Cloudberry S3 Explorer:** This is a Windows tool for managing files between Walrus and S3.

    (c) **s3fs:** This is a FUSE file system, which can be used to mount a bucket from S3 or a Walrus local file system.

    (d) **Vagrant AWS Plugin:** This tool provides configuration files to manage AWS instances and also manage VMs on the local system.

NOTE *You can refer to https://.github.com/eucalyptus/eucalyptus/wiki/ AWS-tools for more information.*

Features of the Eucalyptus Cloud

The following are some of the features of a Eucalyptus cloud:

1. A private cloud is elastic. This means that you can adjust the consumption of its resources per the workload demands of your application.

2. Eucalyptus has AWS API compatibility with Amazon EC2, EBS, S3, IAM, Autoscaling, ELB, and CloudWatch.

3. It provides a user console with hybrid cloud management.

4. Role-based access management.

5. Quota management and accounting.

6. Resource tagging.

7. Customizable instance types.

8. Maintenance mode.

9. High availability.

10. Flexible clustering.

11. Network management.

12. Better security.

13. Traffic management.

14. KVM hypervisor support.

15. MS Windows and Linux guest OS support.

16. VMware hypervisor support.

17. Virtual-to-virtual image conversion (for VMware).

18. Robust Storage Area Network (SAN).

19. OpenStack and Eucalyptus are the two open source cloud software architectures used by organizations all over the world.

20. Eucalyptus operates in four modes: managed mode, managed-n— VLAN mode, static mode, and system mode.

21. Eucalyptus is a system for implementing on-premise private and hybrid clouds using the hardware and software infrastructure that is in place without any modification.

22. It is an add-on capability for data center virtualization to create genuine cloud capability like self-service provisioning, security, performance management, and end-user customizations.

23. Eucalyptus is open source software that can be downloaded for free and it is also shipped with Ubuntu 9.04 and later distributions of Linux.

24. Eucalyptus satisfies the Amazon API syntax.

25. It is compatible with AWS because it provides interfaces like rest and SOAP.

26. The main objective is to present an open source software tool for community sharing which is highly scalable and extensible.

27. Eucalyptus 3.3 was released in June 2013. It includes tools such as autoscaling, ELB, and CloudWatch (a monitoring tool similar to Amazon Cloud watch that supervises resources and applications in Eucalyptus clouds. Eucalyptus 3.3 is the foremost private cloud environment to support Netfix open source tools, which include Edda, Asgard, and Chaos Monkey using API reliability with AWS.

28. Linux-based controller with administrative web portal.

29. EC2-compatible (SOAP, Query).

30. Xen, KVM, and VMware back ends.

Advantages of a Eucalyptus Cloud

The following are some of the advantages of a Eucalyptus cloud:

1. Eucalyptus can be used to achieve the advantages of both public and private clouds.

2. Users can run Amazon or Eucalyptus machine images as instances on both kinds of clouds.

3. It has 100% API compatibility with all AWS services. There are many tools, which are developed to interact seamlessly between AWS and Eucalyptus.

4. Eucalyptus can be used with DevOps tools like Puppet and Chef. Popular SDKs like AWS SDKs for JAVA and Ruby and Fog work smoothly with Eucalyptus.

5. It is not very popular in the market but it is a strong competitor with OpenStack and CloudStack.

There are many IaaS offerings available in the market such as OpenStack, CloudStack, Eucalyptus, and OpenNebula, all of which are being used as both public and private IaaS offerings. Of all the IaaS offerings, OpenStack still remains the most popular, active, and biggest open source cloud computing project; yet enthusiasm for Eucalyptus, CloudStack, and OpenNebula remains solid. Based on critical business requirements, cloud service providers and administrators can choose specific IaaS offerings.

6.9 CLOUD SIM

To meet the challenges of cloud computing (as discussed earlier), CloudSim was introduced. It is an extensible simulation tool kit that facilitates modeling as well as the simulation of cloud computing systems along with application provisioning platforms. This tool kit maintains the systems and behavior modeling of cloud system elements such as data centers, VMs and resource provisioning policies. Some of its main features are as follows:

1. It executes general application provisioning techniques that can be prolonged without difficulty.

2. It also maintains both single and inter-connected clouds.

3. HP labs in the United States are using it to do their research on clouds.

4. The research is on cloud resource provisioning and energy effective management of data center resources.

5. It is very effective because is clear from the scenario that application services are related to dynamic provisioning in the hybrid federated-cloud platform.

SUMMARY

In this chapter, we studied various cloud applications, toolkits, and software for cloud computing. We have also seen the elasticity, extensibility, flexibility, reliability, and applicability of cloud platforms.

CONCEPTUAL SHORT QUESTIONS WITH ANSWERS

Q1. What is AppFabric?

Ans. 1 MS Azure is required to perform services like compute, storage, networking, and identity management. These are tied together by middleware called *AppFabric*.

Q2. What do you mean by MS Azure platform?

Ans. 2 Any application that is built on the Microsoft technology can be scaled using the Azure platform. This integrates the scalability features into a common MS technology such as MS Windows Server 2008, SQL Server, and ASP.NET.

Q3. What is a blob?

Ans. 3 MS Azure allows storing of large amounts of data in the form of Binary Large Objects (BLOBs) by means of the blobs service. This service is optimal for storing large texts of binary files. BLOB storage helps users with the ability to describe the data by adding metadata. It is also possible to take snapshots of a blob for back ups.

Q4. Comment on tables in MS Azure.

Ans. 4. Tables in MS Azure are different from tables in SQL. In this case, tables store unstructured data. There are no rules and schemas either. These are the reasons tables resemble spreadsheets more than SQL tables in RDBMS.

A table can contain up to 100TB of data and rows can have up to 255 properties with a maximum of 1MB for each row. The maximum dimension of row keys and partition keys is 1KB.

Q5. What is geo-replication?

Ans. 5 Geo-replication involves the copy of data into a different data center, which is hundreds or thousands of miles away from the original data center.

Q6. What is Azure Cache?

Ans. 6 It is a service that allows developers to quickly access data persisted on Windows Azure storage or in SQL Azure. This service implements a distributed in-memory cache whose size can be dynamically adjusted by the applications according to their needs. The service is charged according to the size of the cache that is allocated by applications per month. Cache sizes range from 128MB to 4GB.

Q7. Define autonomic cloud bursting and autonomic cloud bridging.

Ans. 7 Autonomic cloud bursting refers to the seamless and secure integration of private enterprise clouds and data centers with public utility clouds on demand to provide the abstraction of resizable computing capacity. For example, CometCloud uses this method.

Autonomic cloud bridging refers to the connection of CometCloud and a virtual cloud, which consists of a public cloud, data center, and grid through the dynamic needs of the application. The clouds in the virtual cloud are heterogeneous and have different types of resources and cost policies. The types of clouds used, the number of nodes in each cloud, and the node resource types should be decided upon according to the changing cloud environments and the application's resource requirements.

Q8. What are the four main components of Yahoo Search?

Ans. 8 The web crawler that downloads pages from web servers; the WebMap that builds a graph of the known web; the Indexer that builds a reverse index to the best pages; and the Runtime that answers users' queries.

Q9. Define a WebMap.

Ans. 9 A WebMap is a graph that consists of roughly 1 trillion edges each representing a web link and 100 billion nodes each representing distinct URLs.

Q10. What is MyLifeBits?

Ans. 10 It was an experiment where an individual's interactions—phone calls, emails, and documents were captured electronically and stored for later access.

Q11. Define volunteer computing.

Ans. 11 Volunteer computing projects work by breaking the problem that they are trying to solve into chunks called *work units*. These are sent to computers all around the world for analysis.

Q12. What are Hadoop Pipes?

Ans. 12 This is the name of the C++ interface to Hadoop MapReduce. Unlike streaming which uses standard input and output to communicate with the map and reduce code, Pipes use sockets as the channel over which the TaskTracker communicates with the process running the C++ map or reduce function. JNI is not used.

Q13. Consider the case study of MAX Hospital. It is a multi-function hospital that has a full complement of facilities. The director of MAX says that "we really wanted to eliminate the drawn-out cycle that people typically face when paying for a doctor's visit and getting compensation for their insurance company." To achieve its goals, MAX decide to create a mobile app that patients can use to:

1. Find doctors based on specialty, location, reviews, and costs.

2. Obtain a detailed invoice at the time of service, which includes all pertinent medical codes and related fees.

3. See how much money their insurance company will pay for service charges.

4. Understand how much money they could save if the provider offers discounts for paying cash on the day of service.

5. Process the payment using their own mobile phone.

Because its app would help facilitate healthcare appointments and payments, MAX decided to design its app as a consumer's single point-of-access to healthcare records and expenses. Therefore, regardless of where people live or what insurance company they use, with the MAX app they can instantly pinpoint when they last had a procedure—such as chicken pox shot—or find out how much they had spent on healthcare over the last 10 years. MAX also decided to create a portal where healthcare providers could enter data about service fees and streamline admissions and check-in processes for registered MAX users. As with any new business idea, success is often closely tied to rapid time-to-market. MAX needed to select, procure, and deploy a completely new infrastructure as quickly and affordably as possible including web servers, storage hardware, and database software. To create a mobile app and portal, engineers also needed to choose a software development platform including a framework and language. The entire solution would need to provide excellent scalability and help simplify compliance with federal healthcare regulations including the Health Insurance Portability and Accountability Act (HIPAA).

Now what should the MAX hospital do? Can the cloud help somewhere?

Ans. 13 Yes. Instead of building its own physical infrastructure, MAX decided to use the cloud. It could now maintain stand-alone infrastructure that was separate from other health centers. The hospital would also be able to get its infrastructure up and running in a few hours and significantly reduce start-up costs and risk, factors that are vital for the success of a company that is still in its infancy stage.

After reviewing current cloud services, MAX chose MS Azure. The reason was that developers were already familiar with the MS platform and development tools including the MS.net framework and MS Visual Studio. With MS Azure, MAX could also take advantage of PaaS (Platform-as-a-Service), IaaS (Infrastructure-as-a-Service), and hybrid cloud options to meet different needs.

For example, to support its mobile app and provider portal, MAX uses many PaaS offerings including MS Azure Cloud Services, Queues, and Service Bus. As a result, developers can focus exclusively on solution development because MS engineers manage the infrastructure. Conversely, engineers use MS Azure Virtual Machines (an offering in IaaS) to control the size and number of their development systems. In the future, if MAX decides to run some systems on-site while keeping others in the cloud, it can do so with the hybrid cloud option in MS Azure.

Soon, developers began to create two versions of its mobile app:

(a) One that runs on the Android OS.

(b) And a second one on iOS.

The mobile app and provider portal are supported by two web roles and one worker role that developers created using the MS Visual C# development tool and the MS Azure SDK:

(a) One web role uses the MS ASP.NET web API framework to expose an API that drives the mobile apps.

(b) Another web role uses MS ASP.NET MVC to support the provider portal.

The worker role facilitates all batch and resource-intensive processing tasks. To support its offerings, the MAX developers use data services in the MS Azure PaaS that include:

(a) MS Azure Tables that contain all personally identifiable information including a subscriber's health history and services in an encrypted format.

(b) MS Azure SQL Database, which contains non-personal metadata.

To simplify development and collaboration, the MAX developers use the MS Visual Studio Team Foundation Server (TFS), which runs on a MS Azure virtual machine. They also use MSTest.exe, a built-in command-line utility in Visual Studio 2013 to customize and run tests.

After one year, MAX launched its mobile app and portal. After one month, MAX had 800 consumers and 10 healthcare providers registered.

NOTE *Developing and running its solution on MS development and cloud platforms, MAX reduced its initial costs, improved its ROI and time-to-market, created a highly scalable solution that gives consumers more insight and control over healthcare costs, and sped compensation cycles for providers.*

CHAPTER REVIEW QUESTIONS

Q1. Distinguish between autonomic cloud bursting and autonomic cloud bridging.

Q2. What is CometCloud?

Q3. What are the benefits of MS Azure?

Q4. What is the MS Azure SQL Database?

Q5. Define AppFabric.

Q6. "Tables in MS Azure are unstructured." Explain.

Q7. What is a BLOB?

Q8. What is Amazon CloudWatch?

Q9. Explain Hadoop.

Q10. Explain MapReduce and its functions.

Q11. Explain Google MapReduce and Hadoop MapReduce.

Q12. Distinguish between RDBMS and MapReduce.

Q13. What are the features of Eucalyptus?

Q14. Summarize Aneka.

Q15. Summarize CloudSim.

APPENDIX **A**

GLOSSARY OF TERMS

1. **Autonomic Computing:** A set of self-managing features of distributed computing resources operating on certain principles.
2. **Chubby:** It maintains sessions between the clients and the servers with the help of keep-alive messages, which are needed every few seconds to remind the system that the session is still active.
3. **Client–Server Architecture:** A form of distributed computing where clients depend on servers for different services and resources.
4. **Cloud API:** A set of programming tools that provides abstractions over a specific cloud provider.
5. **Cloud Computing:** This refers to the technologies that provide compute and application services while the users are unaware of the IT hardware, physical locations, and so on.
6. **Cloud Network:** A network is a connecting link between the user and cloud services.
7. **Cloud Spanning:** Running an application so that its components straddle multiple cloud environments.
8. **Cloud Storming:** The act of connecting multiple cloud computing environments.
9. **Cloud:** A model wherein users have an on-demand access to a shared pool of resources.
10. **Cloudware:** This refers to a variety of software applications at the infrastructure level that enable building, deploying, running, or managing applications in the cloud.

11. **Cluster Controller (CC):** This is a component that is placed on the second level-cluster level of the cloud architecture.

12. **Community Cloud:** A type of cloud that is shared among different organizations with common interests.

13. **Distributed Computing:** This is an implementation technique where different roles or tasks are distributed among separate nodes in the network.

14. **Event-driven SOA:** This is based on the asynchronous exchange of messages among applications and user devices.

15. **Host-based Intrusion Detection Systems (HIDS):** These systems monitors each IaaS host for doubtful activities by analyzing the events within the host.

16. **Identity Management-as-a-Service (IdMaaS):** This is a cloud-based identity management solution that allows users to make use of identity management technologies without spending much on hardware or applications.

17. **Load Balancers:** They can be used to effectively and efficiently manage and spread incoming user traffic among multiple users.

18. **Node Controller:** This is placed at the node level and is executed on all machines that host VM instances.

19. **OpenStack:** This is one among several open-source cloud building software applications through which different companies offer their cloud services to clients.

20. **Ruby-on-Rails:** This is a programming language and Rails is a Ruby framework built for web applications.

21. **SAS 70:** It means Statement on Auditing Standards No. 70, which defines the standards that an auditor must use in order to assess the contracted internal controls of a service provider.

22. **Self-Service Portal:** This is associated with the service catalog that offers an easy-to-use interface for users to select and start using services from within the offered set.

23. **Service Transition:** This is a phase in the IT service life cycle that builds, tests, and deploys a service for operational use.

24. **Snooping:** The access of each tenant should be limited to his/her own data.

25. **SysTrust:** This framework gives cloud service providers a set of pre-defined criteria to evaluate and report their implemented status for security, availability, integrity, and confidentiality of the customer data. This set of criteria is developed by the American Institute of Certified Public Accounts (AICPA) and the Canadian Institute of Chartered Accountants (CICA).

26. **The Open Group (TOG):** TOG has a taskforce called the *Cloud Work Group* with some of the industry's leading cloud providers and end-user enterprises as its members.

27. **Virtualization at the Application Level:** The user-level programs and operating systems are executed on applications that behave like real machines.

28. **Virtualization at the Hardware Abstraction Layer (HAL):** In this virtualization, the time spent in interpreting the instructions issued by the guest platform into the instructions of the host platform is reduced by taking advantage of the similarities that exist between the architectures of the systems.

29. **Virtualization at the Programming Level:** Programming the applications in most systems requires an extensive list of APIs to be exported by implementing different libraries at the user level.

30. **Virtualization:** A process of creating virtual machines or the replicas of computing resources.

31. **VMware Broker:** This is the only optional component in the Eucalyptus cloud and only users who are Eucalyptus subscribers can avail themselves of it.

32. **Vulnerability:** A weakness in system security procedures, system design, or implementation, for example, which could be exploited by a hacker.

33. **Walrus:** It is used by users for storing persistent data in the form of buckets and objects.

34. **XACML:** This is an XML-based language for access control decisions and policy management.

35. **Zeroed:** The degaussing, erasing, or overwriting of electronically stored data.

LAB PROJECTS WITH CLOUD COMPUTING

Project No. 1:	Install and configure Hadoop.
Project No. 2:	Deploy an application as a cloud service using MS Azure.
Project No. 3:	Manage cloud resources.
Project No. 4:	Use existing cloud characteristics and service models.
Project No. 5:	Perform cloud security management.
Project No. 6:	Performance evaluation of services over the cloud.
Project No. 7:	Download an app from the store and create a cloud service that is a custom API to add two numbers.
Project No. 8:	View the list of services and features of the Azure Management Portal.
Project No. 9:	Create a mobile service and access it using the Fiddler tool.
Project No. 10:	Create MS Azure storage and access it via the Azure Explorer tool.
Project No. 11:	Show how the Windows mobile phone and Windows 8 Laptop apps are unified with the help of Azure Cloud Storage.
Project No. 12:	Create a website using Visual Studio 2013 and host it over the Azure portal.
Project No. 13:	Create a VM and host it over the cloud.

ADDITIONAL QUESTIONS FOR DISCUSSION

Q1. Define cloud computing with an example. What are the properties of cloud computing? What is the working principle?

Q2. Define cloud services with an example. In addition, give their advantages.

Q3. List the advantages and disadvantages of cloud computing.

Q4. Name some companies that offer cloud service development.

Q5. What are the issues in web-based applications?

Q6. What is pre-cloud computing?

Q7. Define the following terms:

  (a) Glance

  (b) BLOB

  (c) WiKi

Q8. What is cloud storage? Explain with examples.

Q9. Explain the following:

  (a) SaaS

  (b) PaaS

  (c) IaaS

  (d) DaaS

  (e) Security-as-a-Service

Q10. Discuss different security issues in cloud computing.

Q11. Explain Testing-as-a-Service. What are its different forms? Cloud testing can be done at various levels. Explain these levels.

Q12. Explain Integration-as-a-Service.

Q13. Write a short summary of "Cast Iron Cloud."

Q14. What is Hadoop?

Q15. What are the features of Eucalyptus?

Q16. What is MapReduce? Explain in detail.

Q17. Explain the technologies and the tools used for cloud computing.

Q18. Explain the following:

    (a) Autonomic cloud bursting

    (b) Autonomic cloud bridging

Q19. Explain paravirtualization.

Q20. Define the following:

    (a) Data lineage

    (b) Data Remanence

    (c) Replication

    (d) Clustering

    (e) ACID

    (f) Cloud Data Centers

    (g) SLAs

    (h) Eucalyptus

    (i) CloudSim

Q21. Explain different cloud architectures.

Q22. How has the cloud evolved over the last several years? Explain.

Q23. Explain cloud testing in detail.

Q24. Do you face any challenges during cloud testing?

Q25. What are different types of clouds?

Q26. Give different cloud security challenges.

Q27. Explain the role of a hypervisor or VMM.

Q28. What is mobile cloud computing? Discuss its architecture with a clear diagram.

Q29. The features of MS Azure are as follows:

(a) Compute

(b) Data services

(c) App services

(d) Network services

(e) Commerce

Explain each of these features with respect to MS Azure.

Q30. What is the latest mantra Microsoft is using to describe devices and services?

Q31. Explain cloud federation and characterize it.

Q32. Distinguish between the following:

(a) Private and public clouds.

(b) Public and hybrid clouds.

(c) Private and community clouds.

(d) Buffering and caching.

(e) Cloud bursting and cloud bridging.

(f) Horizontal and vertical scaling.

(g) PaaS, IaaS, and SaaS.

(h) MapReduce and RDBMS.

(i) Cloud bursting and cloud sourcing.

(j) Traditional data center and cloud data center.

(k) CA and CRLs.

(l) Digital certificates and digital signatures.

(m) Map() and Reduce() functions.

(n) Thin provisioning and cloud provisioning.

(o) Google MapReduce and Hadoop MapReduce.

(p) Eucalyptus versus other IaaS Private clouds.

Q33. What are the issues related to Cloud Data Centers (CDCs)?

Q34. What are autonomic systems? Discuss some of their features.

Q35. Explain cloud business-process management with a clear diagram.

Q36. What is a cloud stack?

Q37. Write short summaries for:

    (a) Cloud governance

    (b) Cloud analytics

    (c) Cloud sourcing

    (d) Cloud provisioning

    (e) Cloud virtualization

Q38. Explain the bare-metal and hosted virtualization architectures with clear diagrams.

Q39. Explain virtualization under the following headings:

    (a) Server virtualization

    (b) Storage virtualization

    (c) Network virtualization

    (d) Service virtualization

    (e) Desktop virtualization

Q40. Why are Type-1 VMMs better in performance than Type 2 VMMs?

Q41. What are the limitations of paravirtualization, hardware emulation, and OS virtualization?

Q42. Write short summaries for:

    (a) VMware ESXi

    (b) Xen

    (c) KVM

    (d) Elasticity

    (e) Eucalyptus

    (f) OpenNebula

    (g) Energy issues at CDCs

Q43. Researchers say that there is a need to play with the energy cards at cloud data centers. What possible solutions do you propose to minimize energy consumption?

Q44. How will you select the deployment models?

Q45. Explain Porter's model for ECC with diagrams.

Q46. Q46. What is a cloud supply chain?

Q47. What is the amplification rule for web security vulnerability?

Q48. Write short summaries of:

    (a) Throwaway clouds

    (b) Federated clouds

    (c) CometCloud

Q49. What are the advantages of a Eucalyptus cloud?

Q50. Explain the following Eucalyptus terminology:

    (a) Images

    (b) Instances

    (c) Networking

    (d) Access control

    (e) Eucalyptus EBS

    (f) Autoscaling and Load Balancing

Q51. What other tools exist that can interact with Eucalyptus?

Q52. Explain Aneka?

[Hint: Aneka binds the system resources of a diverse network of workstations as well as servers or data centers based on need. It has a set of APIs for developing these resources. It is a .net-based service-oriented resource management and development platform. Each server in an Aneka deployment hosts the Aneka container that provides the base infrastructure that consists of services for persistence, security, and communication. It is a software platform and a framework for developing distributed applications on the cloud. It harnesses the computing resources of a heterogeneous network of workstations and servers or data centers on demand. It is an implementation of the PaaS model. Aneka is a flexible, extensible market-oriented cloud application development and deployment solution. It allows servers and desktops PCs to be linked together to form a very powerful computing infrastructure].

REFERENCES

[1] Chopra, Rajiv. 2016. *Web Engineering*, 1st ed., Eastern Economy Edition (EEE). India: Prentice-Hall of India, Pvt. Ltd.

[2] Chopra, Rajiv. *Testing Web Applications: The State of Art and Future Trends*. Cambridge, UK: Cambridge International Science Publishing.

[3] Rao, M. N. 2015. *Cloud Computing*. Prentice Hall.

[4] Raj Kumar Buyya, Rajiv and Anirban Basu. 2012. Proceedings of the Conference "Advances in Cloud Computing," 26–28 July.

[5] Jayaswal, Kailas, et al. 2014. *Cloud Computing: Black Book*. Dreamtech Press.

[6] Hurwitz, Judith, et al. 2015. *Cloud Computing for Dummies*. Wiley.

[7] Chee, Brian J. S., et al. 2014. *Cloud Computing*, CRC Press.

[8] Chopra, Rajiv and Kapila Kapoor. 2007. "Test Point Analysis—A Black Box Test Effort Estimation Technique." National Conference on Trends in Computing (NCTC), 18–19 May, pp. 444.

[9] Rajiv Chopra and Kapila Kapoor. 2009. "Regression Testing of Relational Databases." *INDIACOm-2009*, 26–27 Feb., pp. 423–424, 432.

[10] Chopra, Rajiv and Sushila Madan. 2013. "Reusing Existing Black Box Test Paths for White Box Testing of Websites." 3rd IEEE International Advance Computing Conference [IACC], *IEEE Digital X'plore Library*, India, Feb. 22–23, pp. 1339–1350.

[10] Chopra, Rajiv and Sushila Madan. 2013. "Symbiotic Association between Cyber Security and Website Testing." International Conference on Diversifying Trends in Technology and Management [CTI-Con], April 6–7, pp. 1–5. India: *International Journal of Technology and Management.*

[11] Chopra, Rajiv and Sushila Madan. 2013. "The Laws of Cyber Security and the Maturity Model." 7th International Conference on Advanced Computing and Communication Technologies (ICACCT 2013), Nov. 16, pp. 31–33. IETE and Computer Society IEEE, Delhi section. India: *InderScience Publishers.*

[12] Chopra, Rajiv. 2015. "Testing a Day, Keeps Errors at Bay." 4th International Conference on Progressing Towards Responsible Economy: Issues and Perspectives, Jan. pp. 187–192.

[13] Chopra, Rajiv. 2015. "Web Security, Internet Security and Cyber Security: A Report." 2nd International Conference on Emerging Trends of Engineering, Science, Management and its Applications (ICETESMA-15), Proceedings published by *Pearson Inc.,* Vol. 4, Special Issue, Mar., pp. 18–22.

[14] Chopra, Rajiv. 2015. "Security during Secure Software Development Life Cycle." International Conference on Engineering Technology, Management and Applied Sciences (ICETMAS-15), Proceedings published by *McGraw Hill* (MGH), Vol. 1, Special Issue, Sept., pp. 1–4.

[15] Chopra, Rajiv. 2015. "Parameterized Gray Box Testing with Graph-TreeGen Tool." International Conference on Engineering Technology, Science and Management Innovation (TSMI-15), Proceedings published by *Pearson Inc.,* Vol., Special Issue, Mar., pp. 8–20.

[16] Chopra, Rajiv. 2016. "Cyber Tsunami: A Report." 4th International Conference on Imperatives of Global Business: Innovation and Knowledge Management (ICBIK-16), Proceedings published by *Bloomsbury Publications, London,* Feb. 11–12, pp. 305–316,

[17] Rajiv Chopra and Sushila Madan. 2012. "Testing Websites Using $P^3 R^2$ Model." *International Journal of Computer Science Issues* (IJCSI), Vol. 9, Issue 4, July, pp. 248–253.

[18] Chopra, Rajiv and Sushila Madan. 2012. "A Practical T-P^3R^2 Model to Test Dynamic Websites." *Journal of Information Engineering and Applications* (JIEA), IISTE, Vol. 2, No. 6, July, pp. 44–47.

[19] Chopra, Rajiv and Sushila Madan. 2012. "Analysis and Security Testing of Websites Using P³R² Model." *Cyber Times International Journal of Technology & Management* (CTIJTM), Vol. 5, No. 1, Oct. 2011–March 2012, pp. 1–18.

[20] Chopra, Rajiv and Sushila Madan. 2012. "Analysis of Various Path Testing Tools for Websites." *Vikas International Journal of Management, Science and Technology*, (VIJMST), Vol. 1, Issue 1, Jan.–June. pp. 1–4.

[21] Chopra, Rajiv and Sushila Madan. 2015. "Locating a Pin in a Haystack before the Customer Finds." *International Journal of Applied Information Systems* (IJAIS), linked to *Harvard University*, Vol. 8, No. 2, Jan., pp. 47–49.

[22] Chopra, Rajiv. 2015. "Web Security, Internet Security and Cyber Security: A Report." *International Journal of Innovations and Advancement in Computer Science* (IJIACS), Vol. 4, Special Issue, Mar., pp. 18–22.

[23] Chopra, Rajiv. 2015. "Challenges of Website Testing." *International Journal of Innovations and Advancement in Computer Science* (IJIACS), Vol. 4, Special Issue, May, pp. 12–15.

[24] Chopra, Rajiv. 2015. "Security during Secure Software Development Life Cycle." *International Journal of Engineering Technology, Management and Applied Sciences* (IJETMAS), Vol. 3, Special Issue, Sept., pp. 1–4.

INDEX